I love animals. I love them mainly for their innocence, and I love photographing them for many other reasons, such as their beauty, colors, textures, uniqueness, form, etc.; and naturally, for their expressions.

Sometimes, if one is very observant, many creatures will display a range of expressions that are very similar to ours. These can be very fleeting, but if your finger is ready on the shutter, and your eye is following their every move, they can be captured for all time.

Of course, the human-like expressions come from the apes and monkeys, but just about any of them can convey an attitude, a pose, or a certain look that can well be termed as a "communicative moment."

Sometimes, their photographs need no comment at all, just their presence is more than enough, even with no discernible expression. But I especially enjoy it when they seem to be saying something, that to me, looks very expressive and funny. At those times, I just can't help but imagine a caption for my thoughts. I like to think that if they could reason and go along with this, they would certainly love to be in on the game.

About Dan Barba, photographer:

Originally having practiced as an Engineer, and not finding the work fulfilling, I picked up the photo hobby, or 'bug.'

Eventually, I ended up as a full time pro photographer in South Florida. Soon thereafter I moved to Manhattan, NY with my wife, Olga. There, I worked with the leading Advertising Agencies, corporations and magazines, initially shooting fashion and beauty and later on, large format still life commercials for single ads and/or campaigns.

Working with Advertising/commercial clients is extremely demanding and competitive, with many creative restraints, and the equipment/business investments considerable, although the financial rewards are great. One has to execute very specific photo layouts exactly how the concept demands and a lot of money can be involved in the project. So, it's got to be done right, the first time. All the while, appearing as cool as possible. Wheew!

On any given day in my studio, there could have been an Art/Creative Director from the Ad Agency, any number of clients, attorneys, client/account representatives, an Art Buyer, models, prop and make-up/hair stylists plus several assistants, not to mention my Agent. That is a lot of people intruding on one's private mental world. It is highly intense and it can only be done sanely for a given number of years. Some photographers can do it indefinitely, but many don't even try; nor should they, I believe. I certainly didn't.

So at one point, after a fruitful career, I retired. But I continue to shoot (for myself only) personal creative work, which is what I originally went into photography for. No more creative constraints now. Anything that strikes my eye is game. This is what really fulfills me, and not only shooting pictures, but hand-holding them all the way to the finished concept through the wonderful medium of today's digital workflow.

Now, I would like to share this small collection with all those with an appreciative eye.

No animals have been retouched in this book. All expressions are original and real.
Only color correction, dust removal & cropping have been done.

© 2012 by Dan Barba

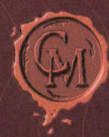

A CM BOOK

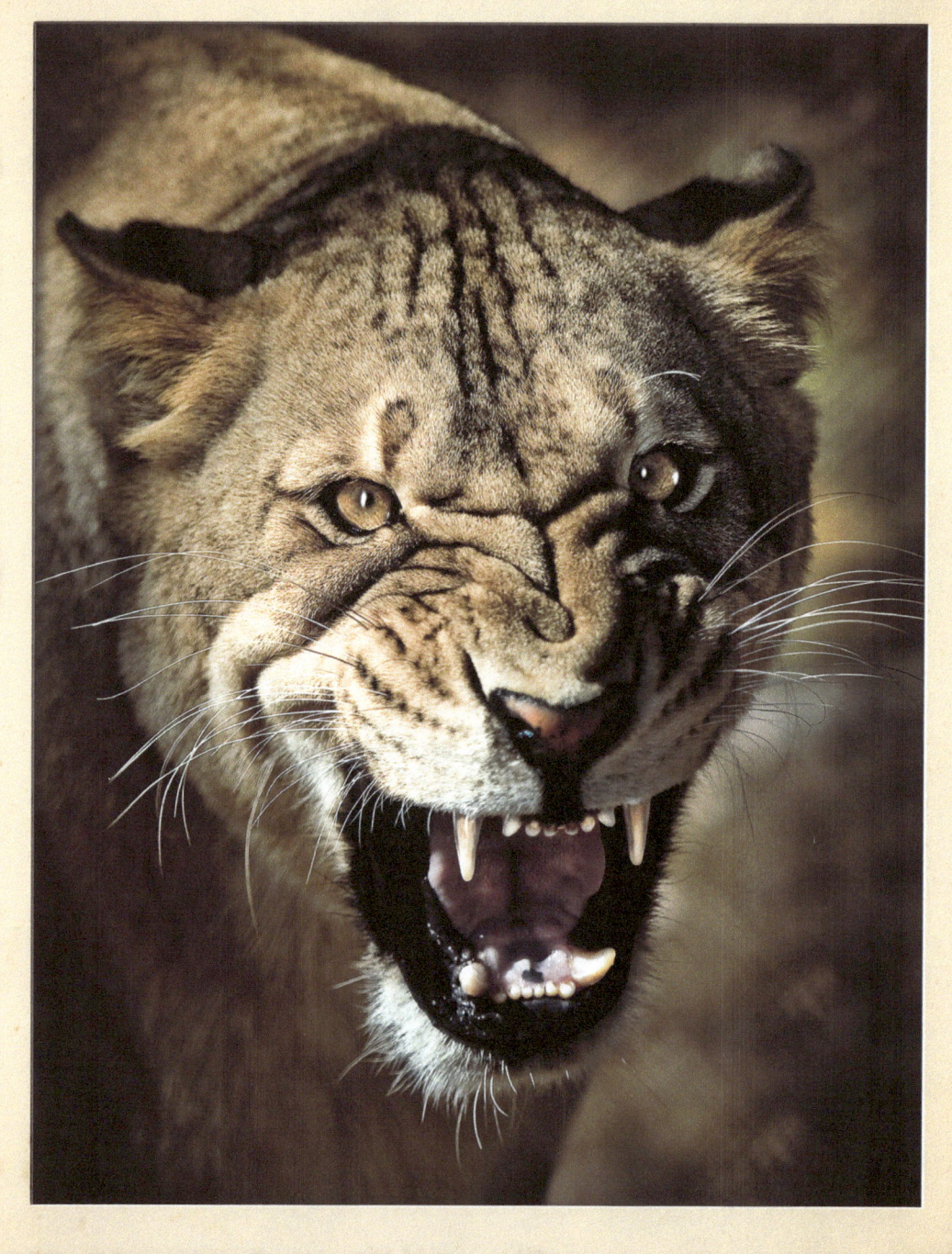

Hello, Mr. Photographer,
...very pleased
to Eat you...

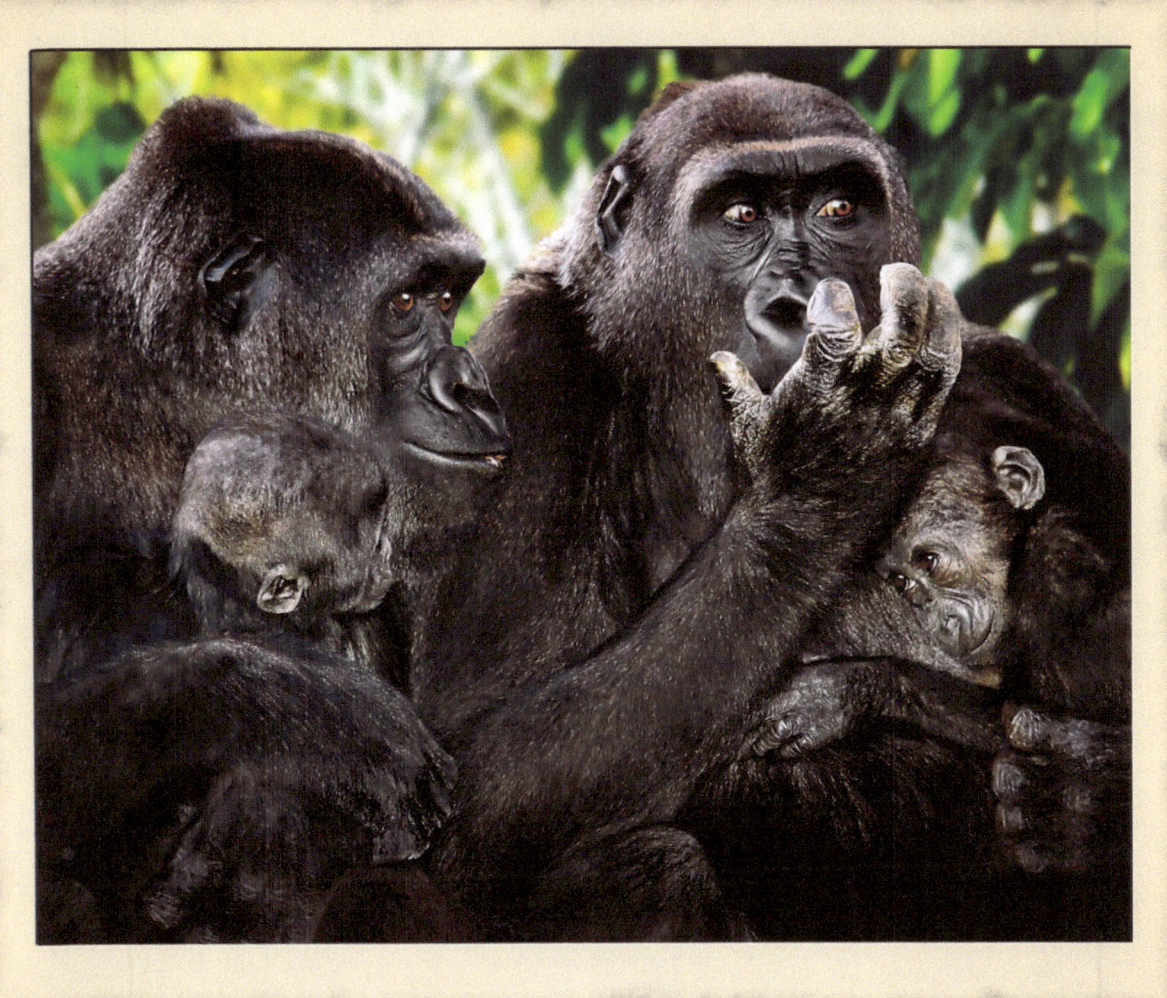

Say Agnes, is that Randy
with a banana, or is he
just happy to see us?...

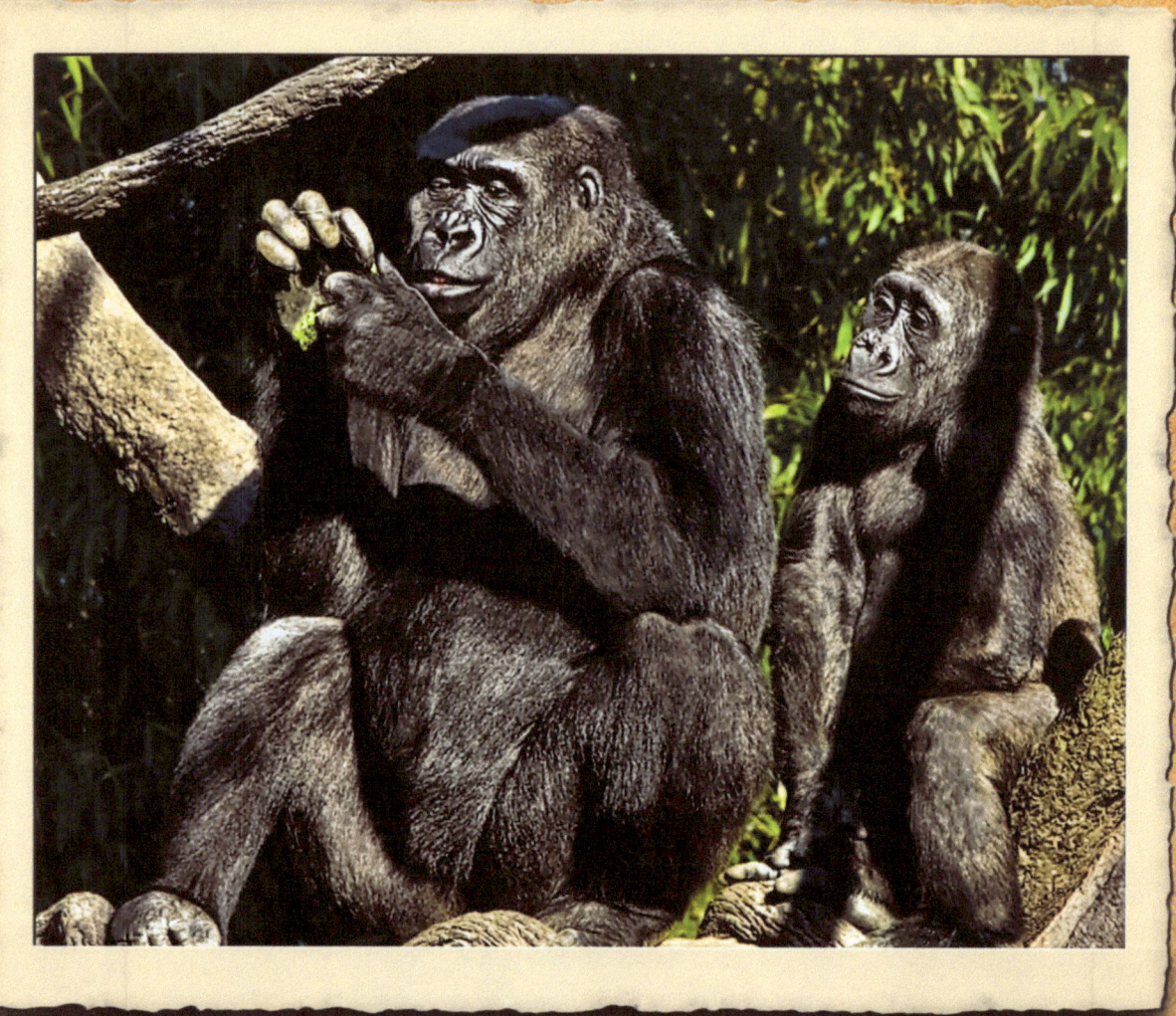

You see Junior,
back in My day...

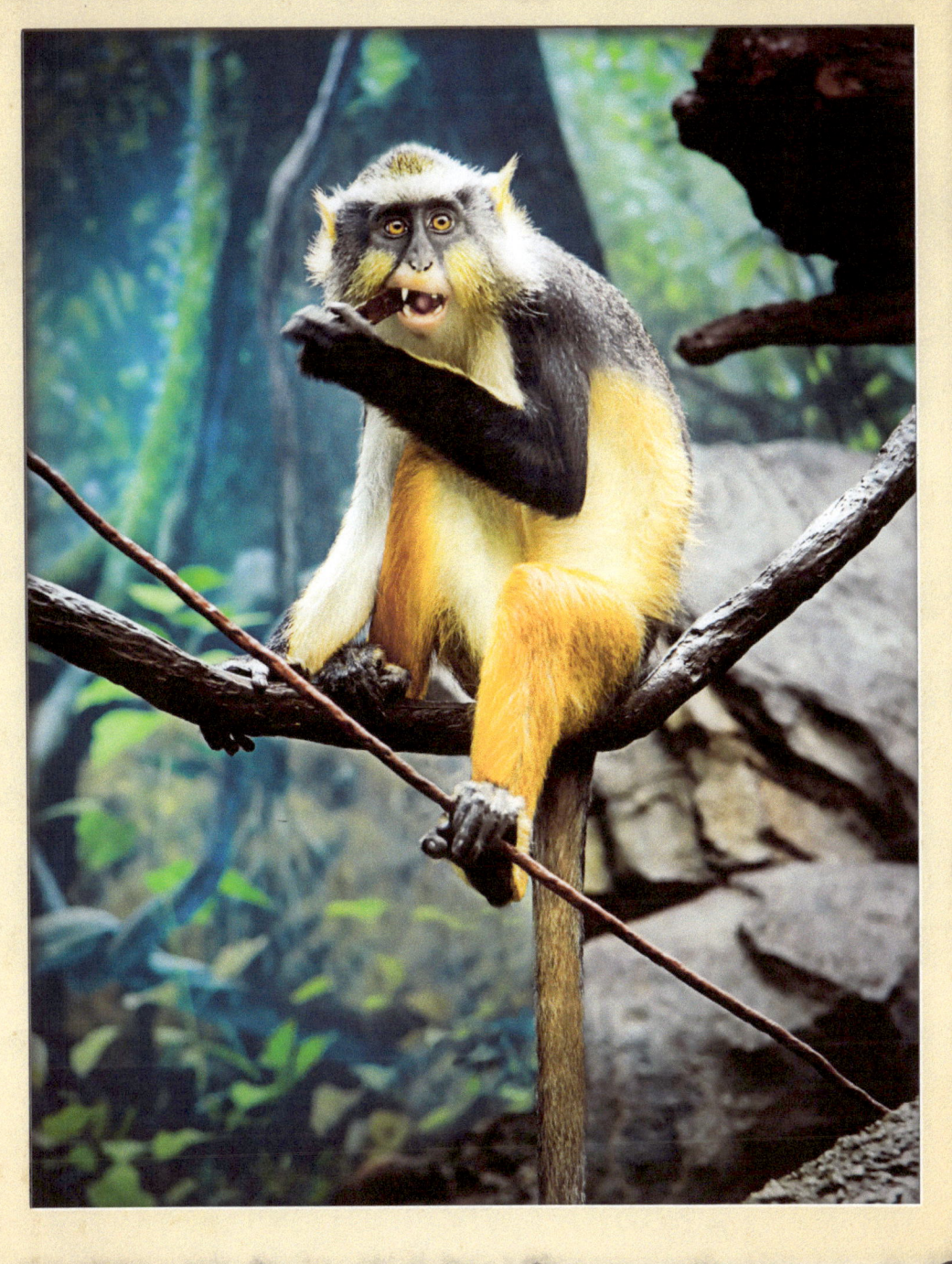

Me? Oh, you know,
just hanging around
chewing the fat...

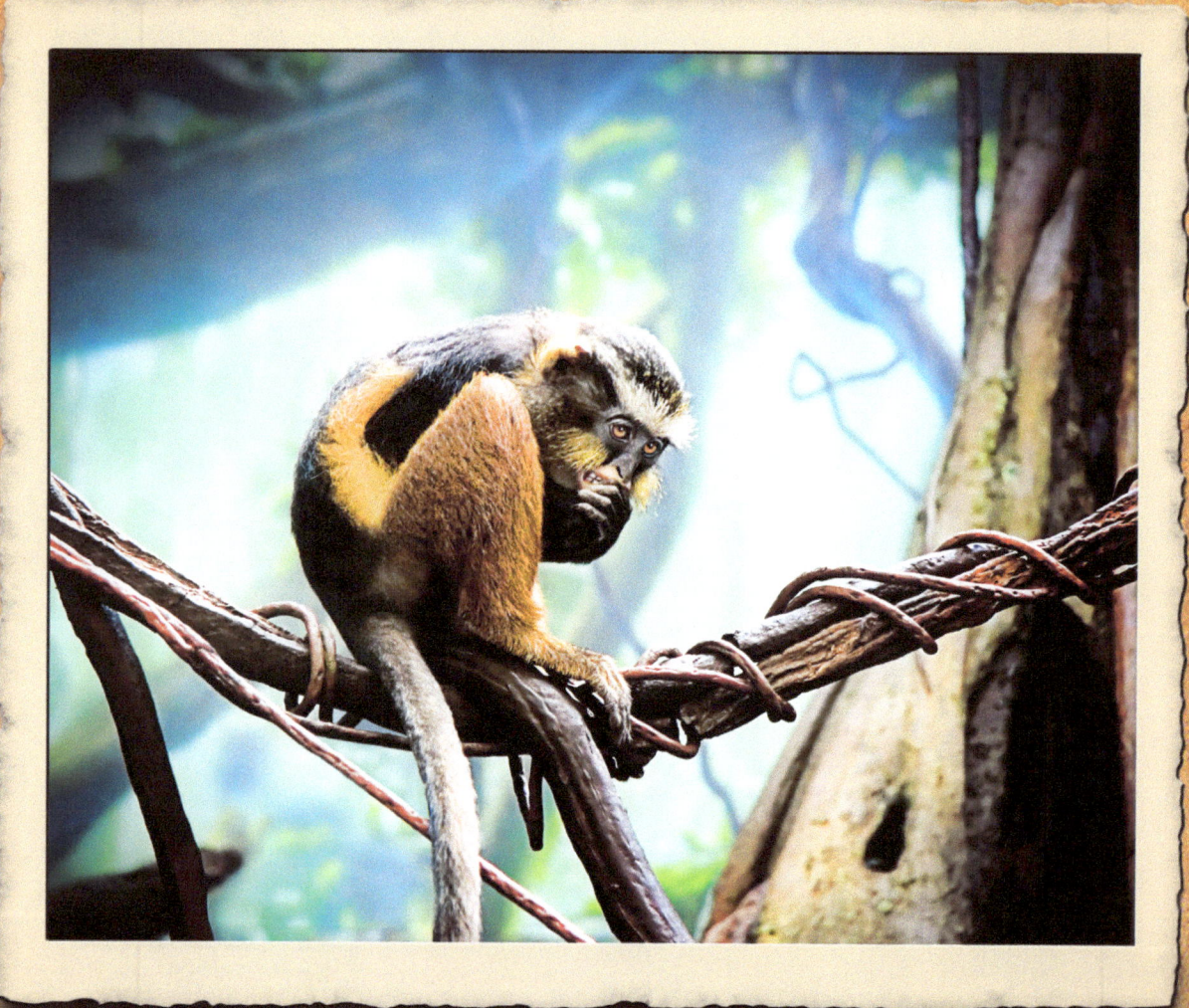

I wonder who that evil Henderson kid will pick on next...

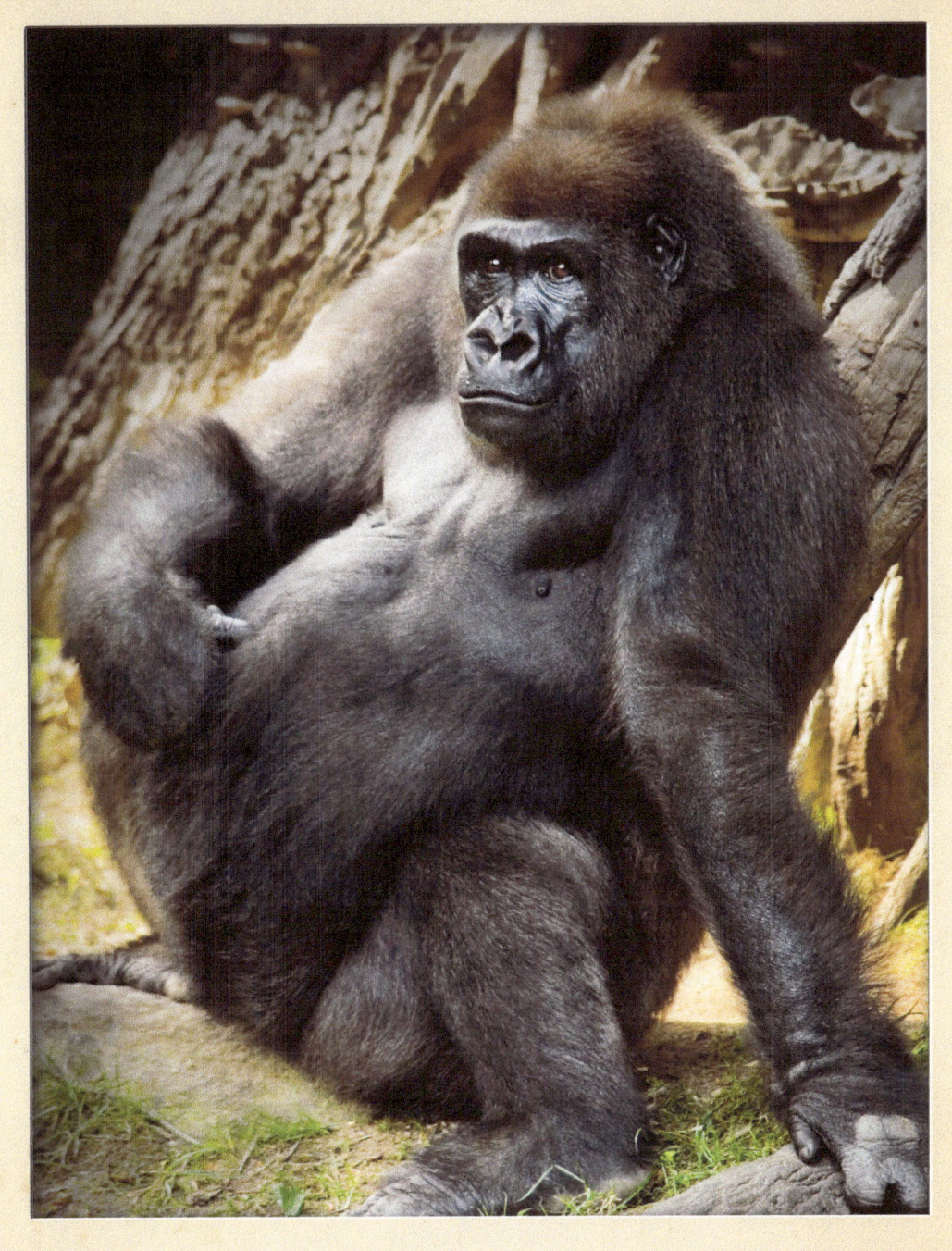

I'm strenously striving to
become that mythical
800 lb. Gorilla...

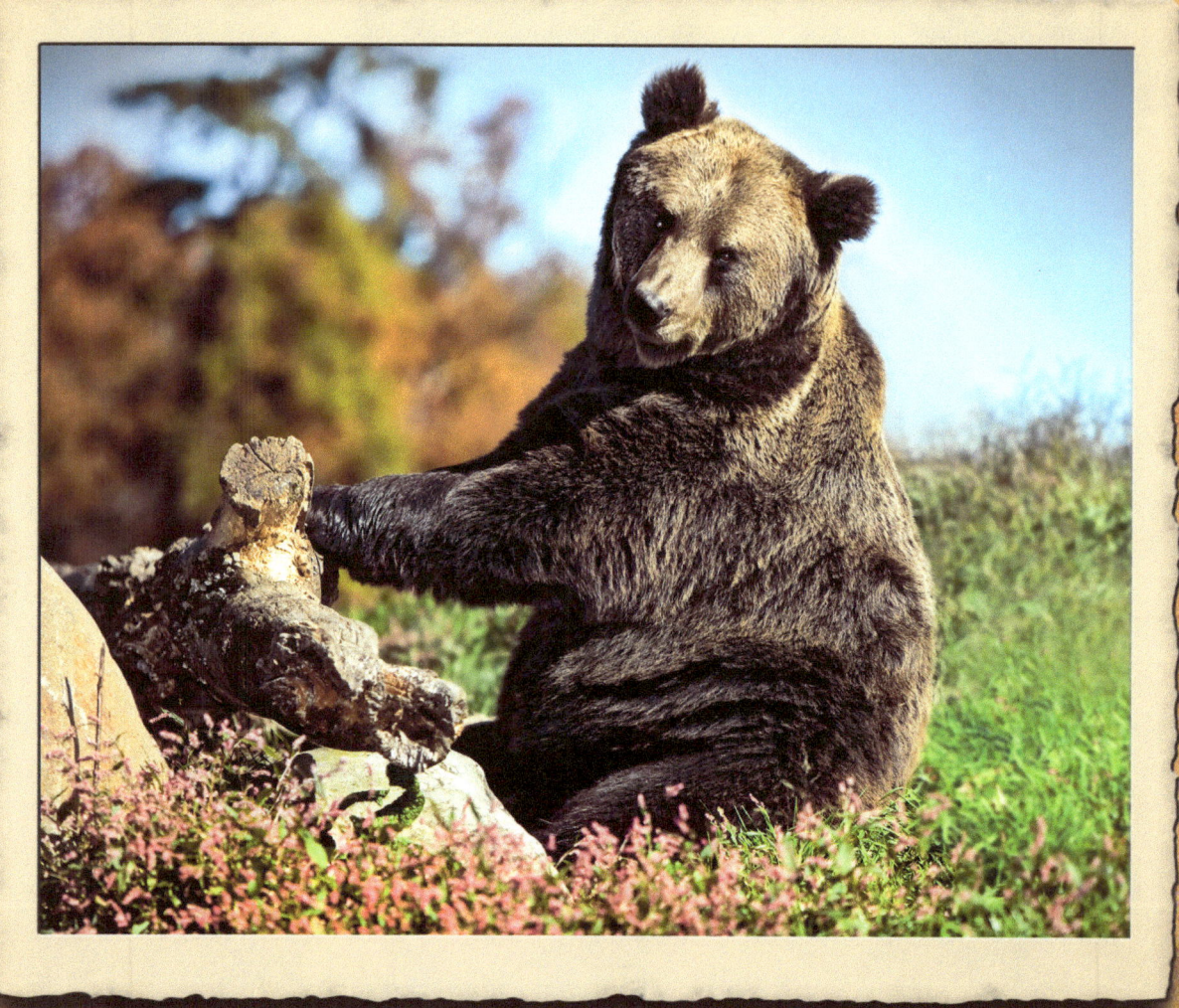

Is this coquettish
enough for you,
Mr. Photographer?...

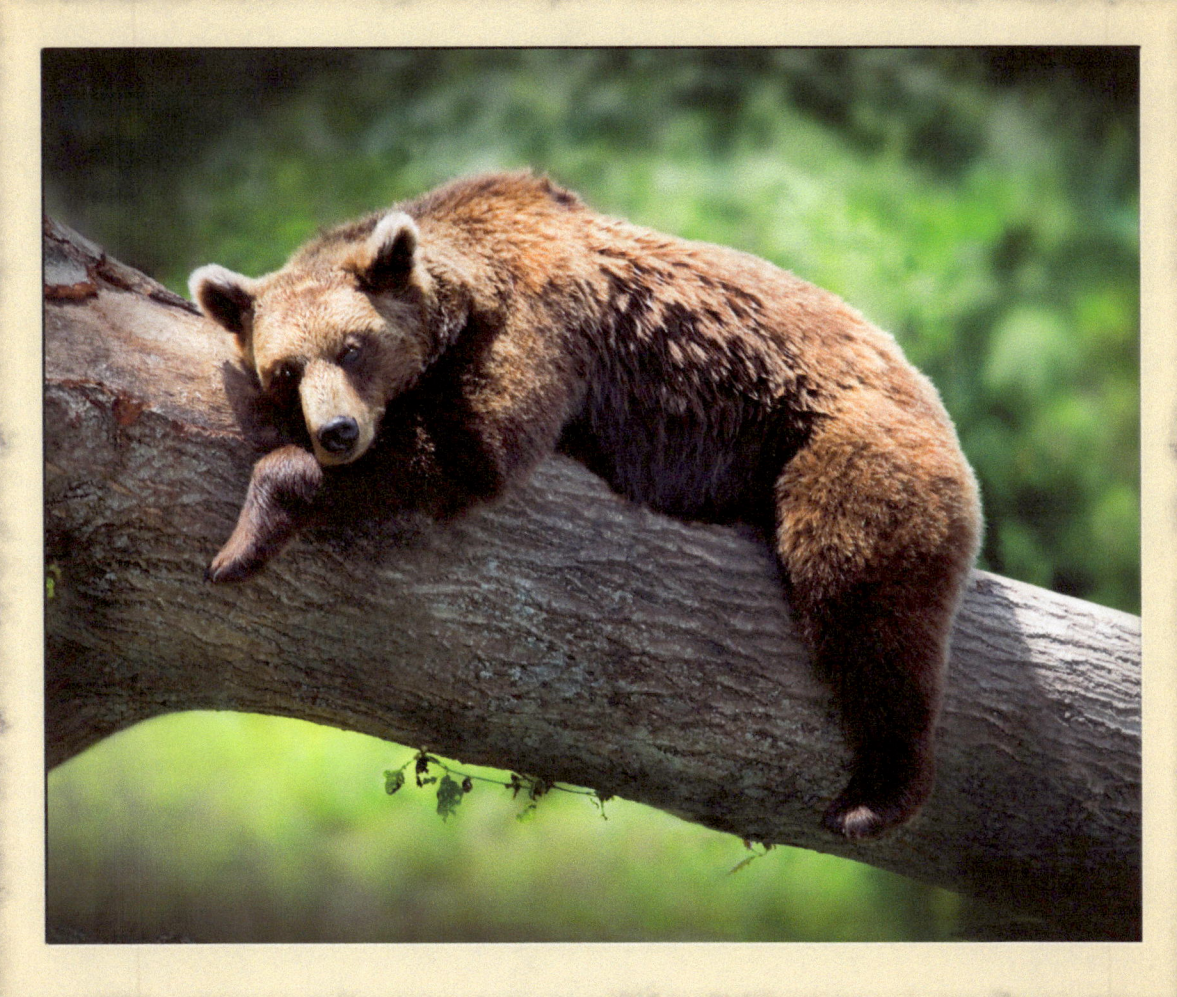

Oh, I dunno, there's gotta be more
to the meaning of life than just
being promoted to 'Branch Manager'...

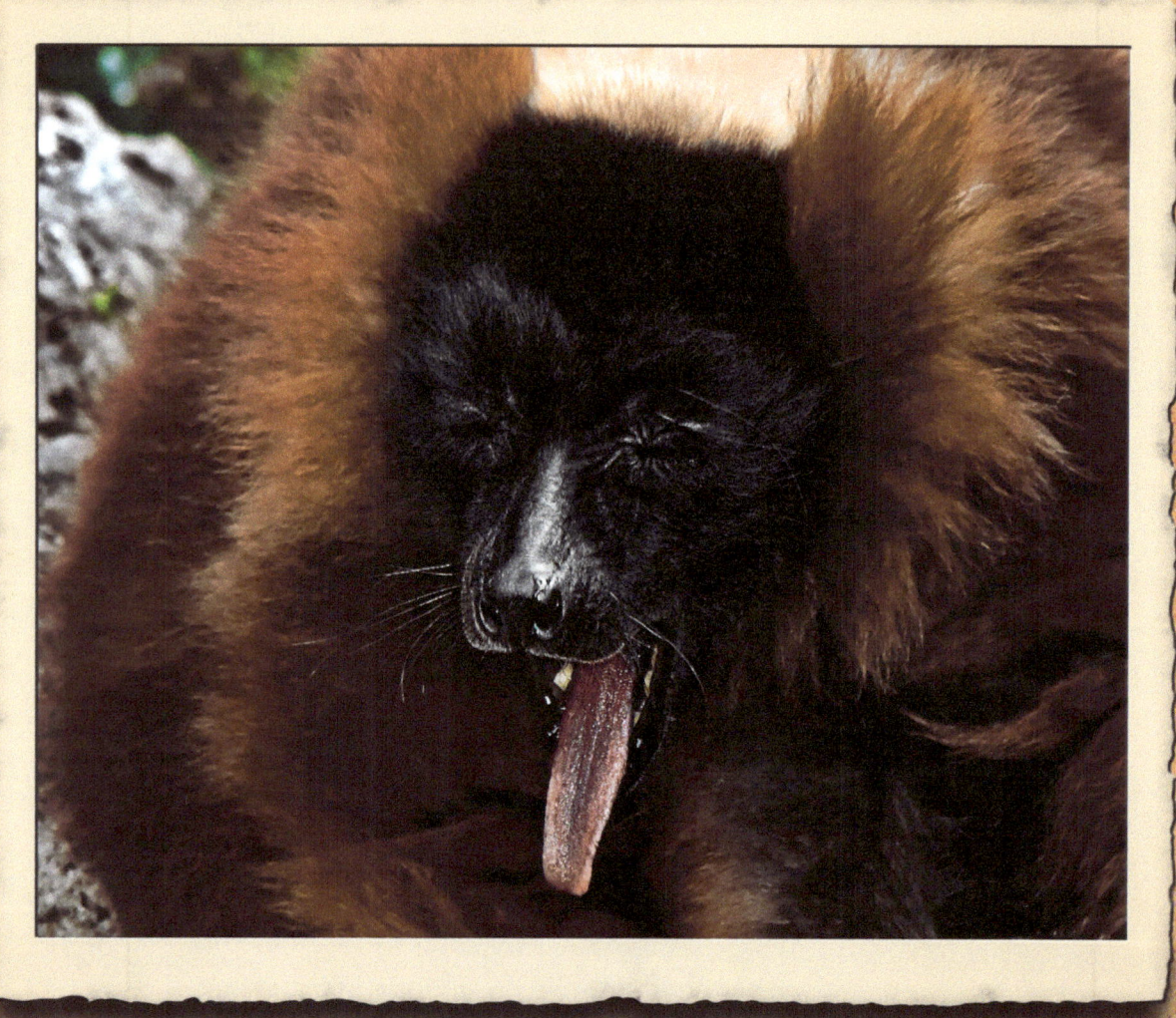

Hairball
of the Wild

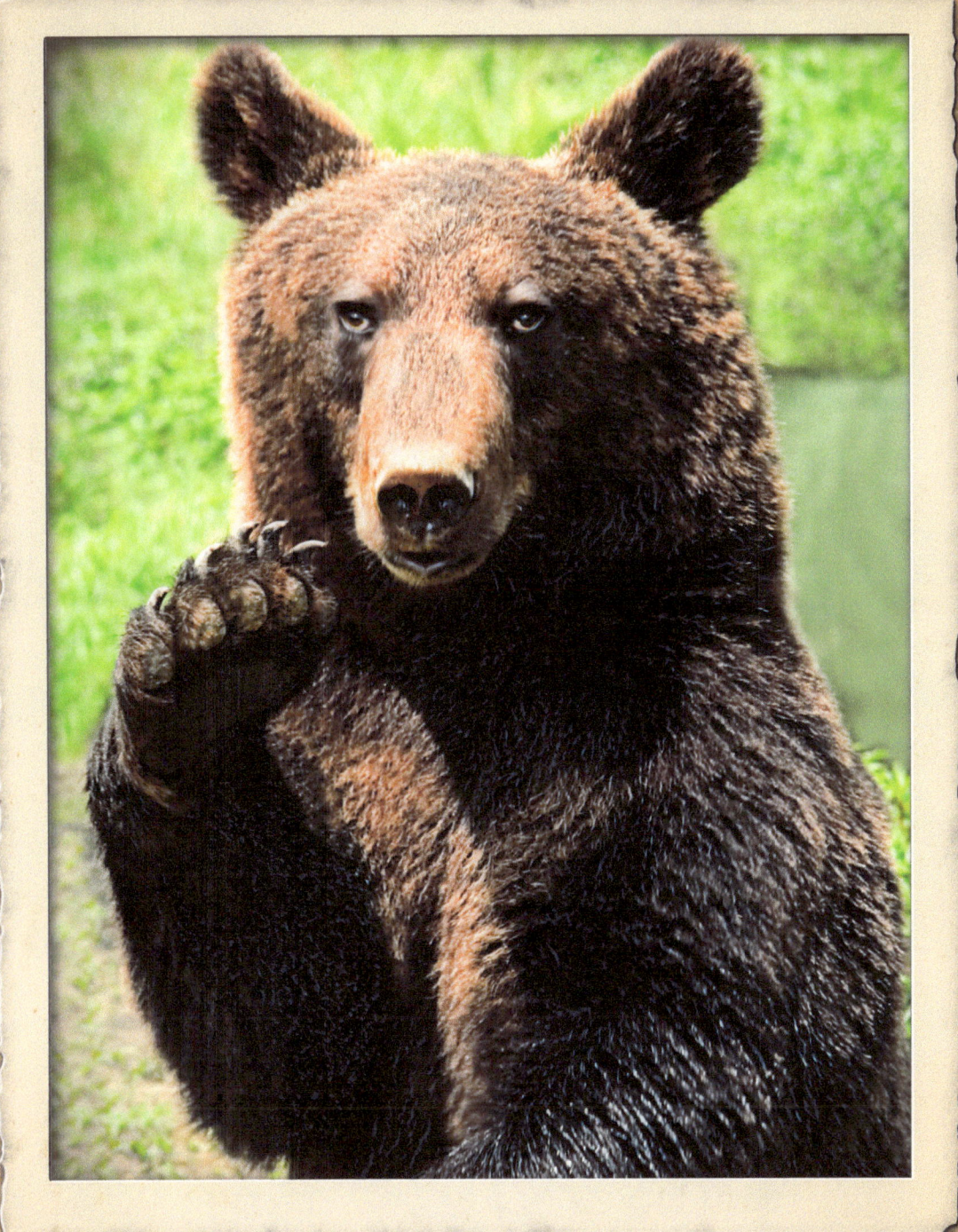

I will kill you all with my
Kung-Fu prowess,
you dirty bastards!!!

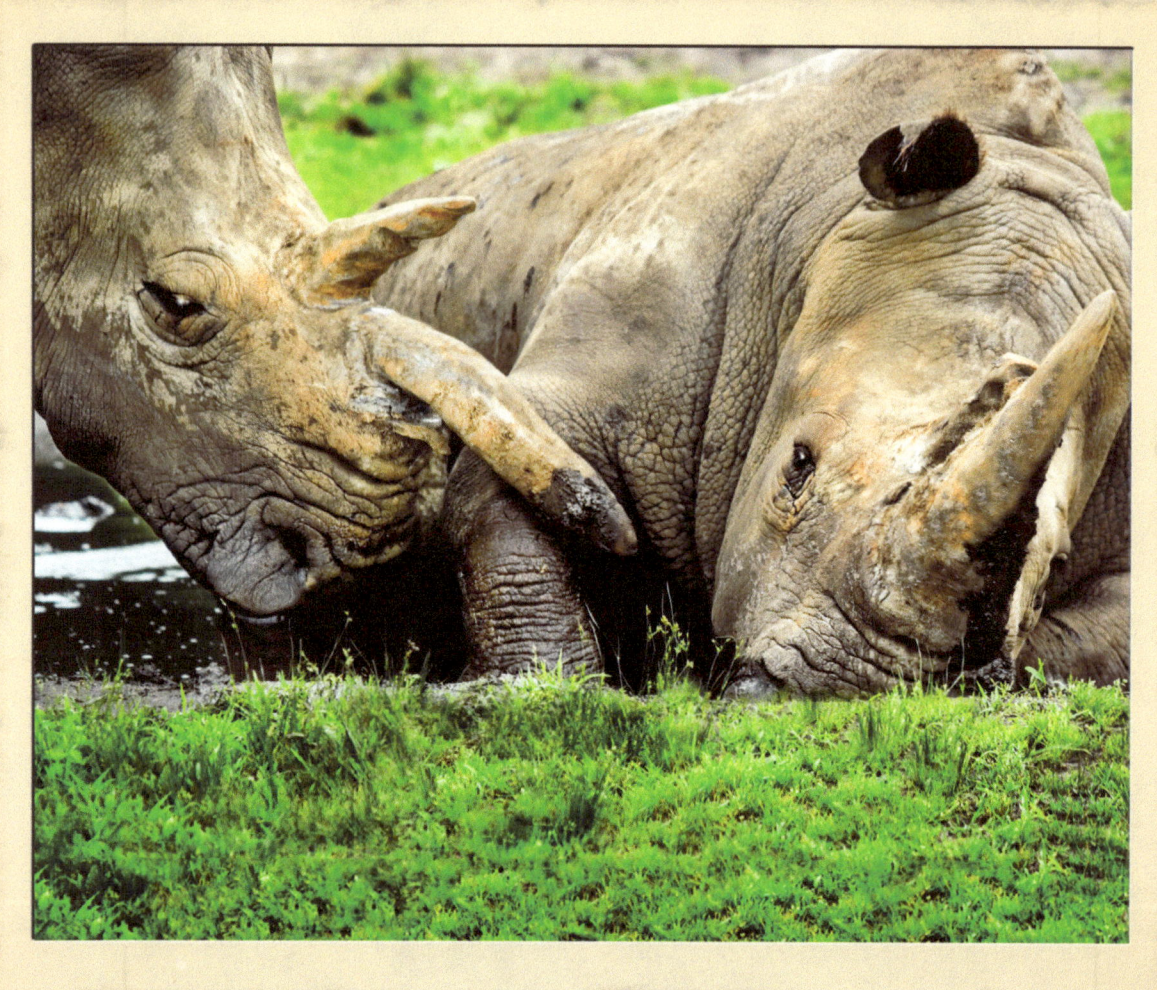

Now Doreen, I know I'm not the Rhino I used to be, but I promise to take one of them new-fangled pills next time...

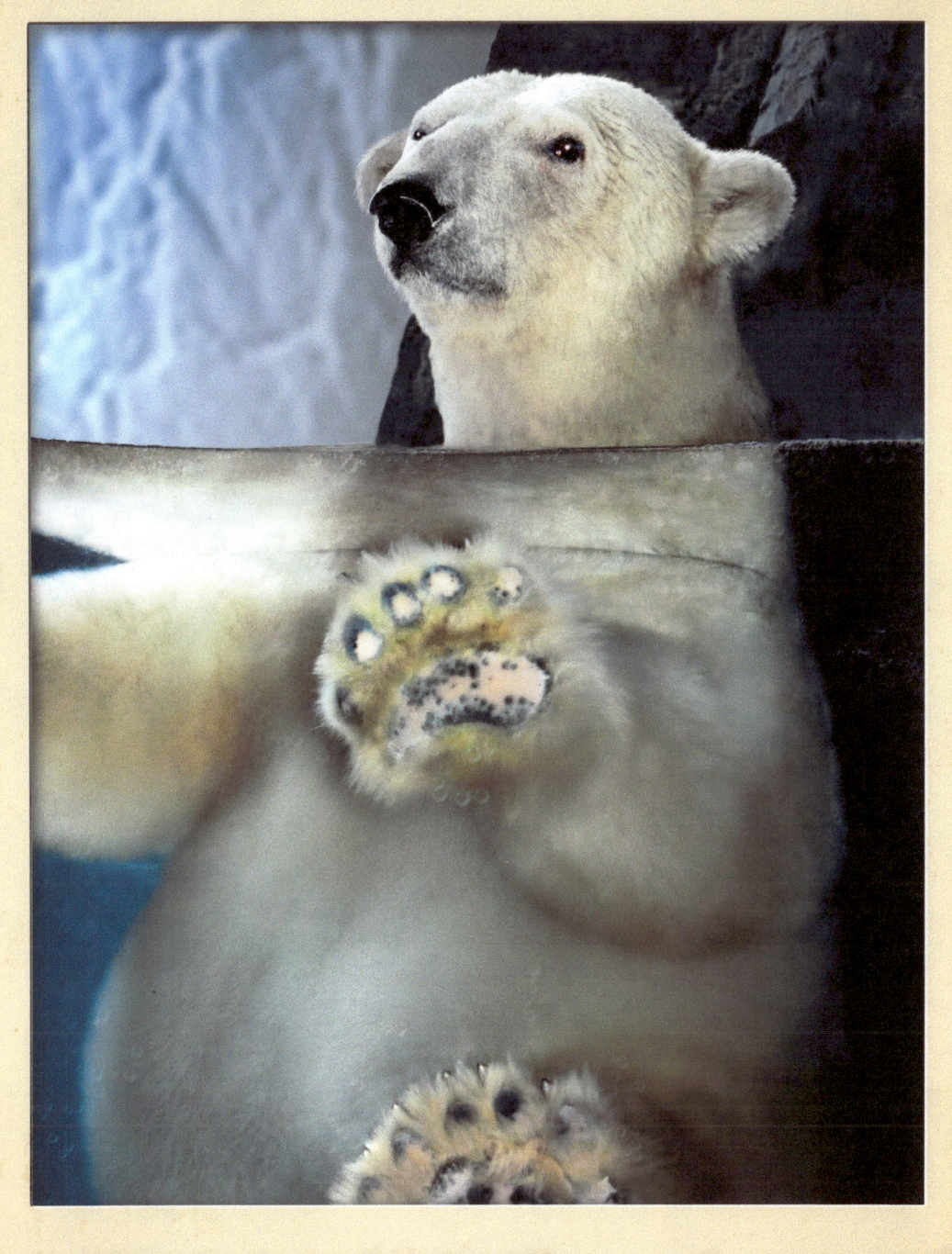

Y'know, every time I bathe,
I sense all these eyes
watching, undressing me...

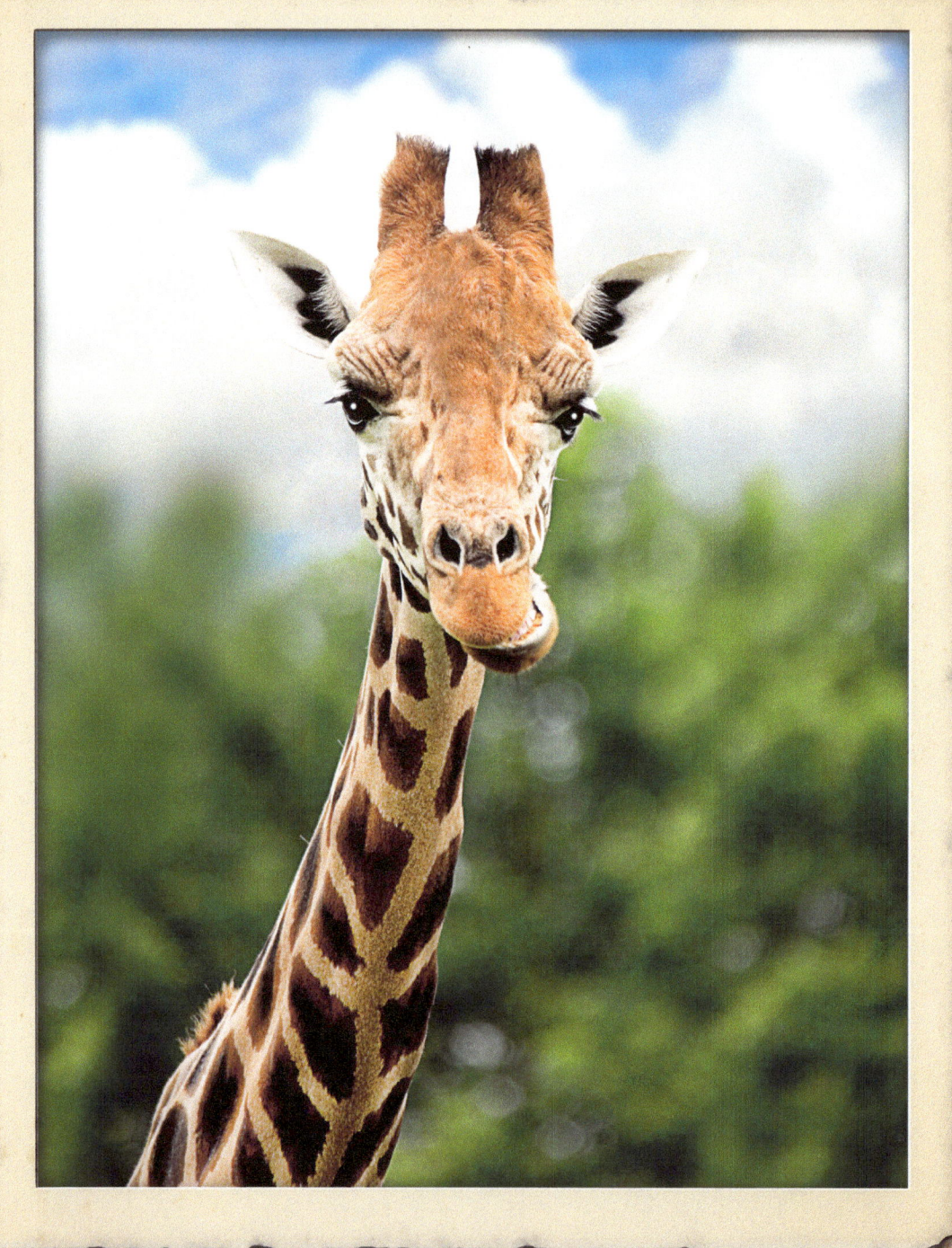

I know I ain't pretty,
but I do boast a
long and svelte neck line...

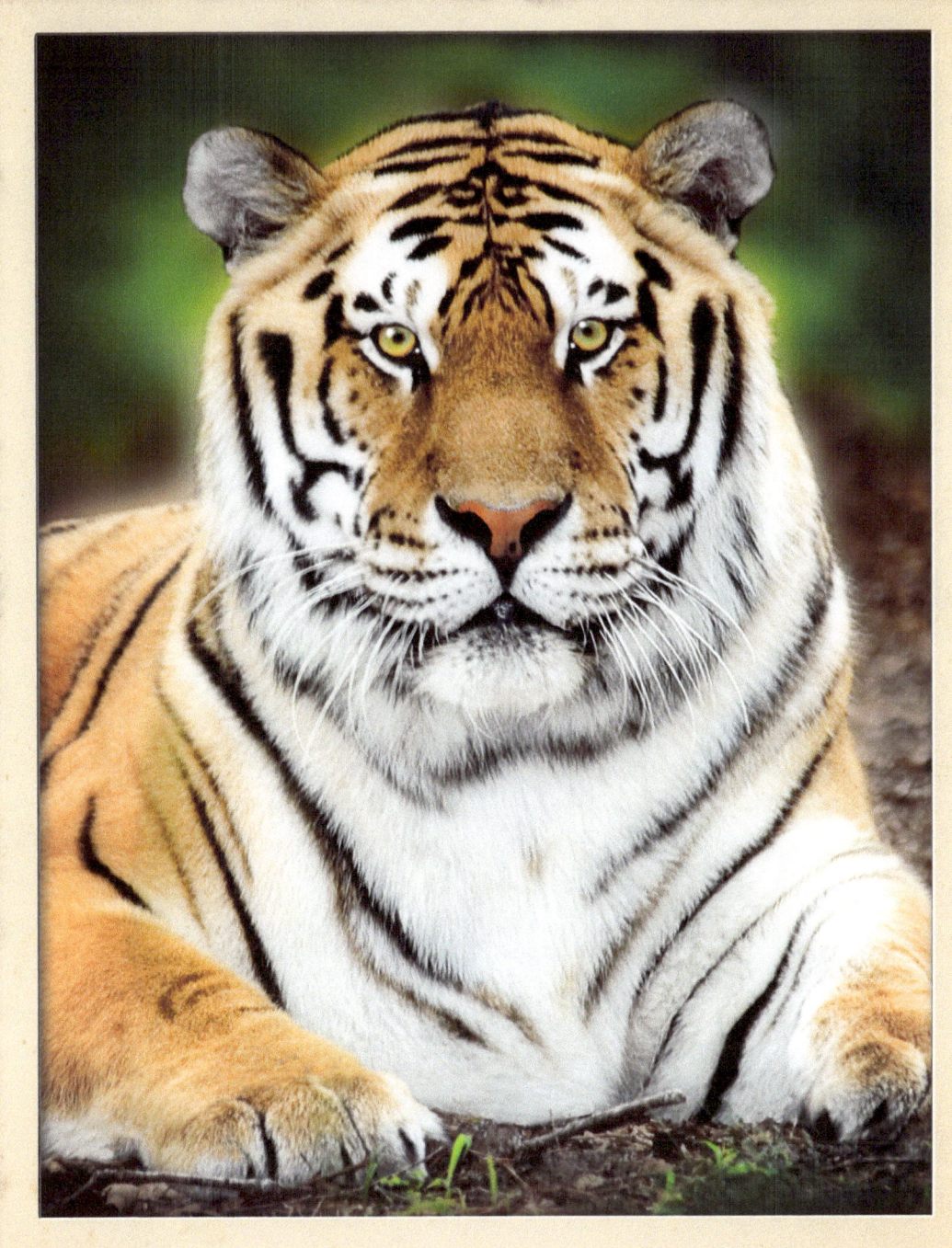

Don't bother me now,
I'm concentrating
on my Mantra...

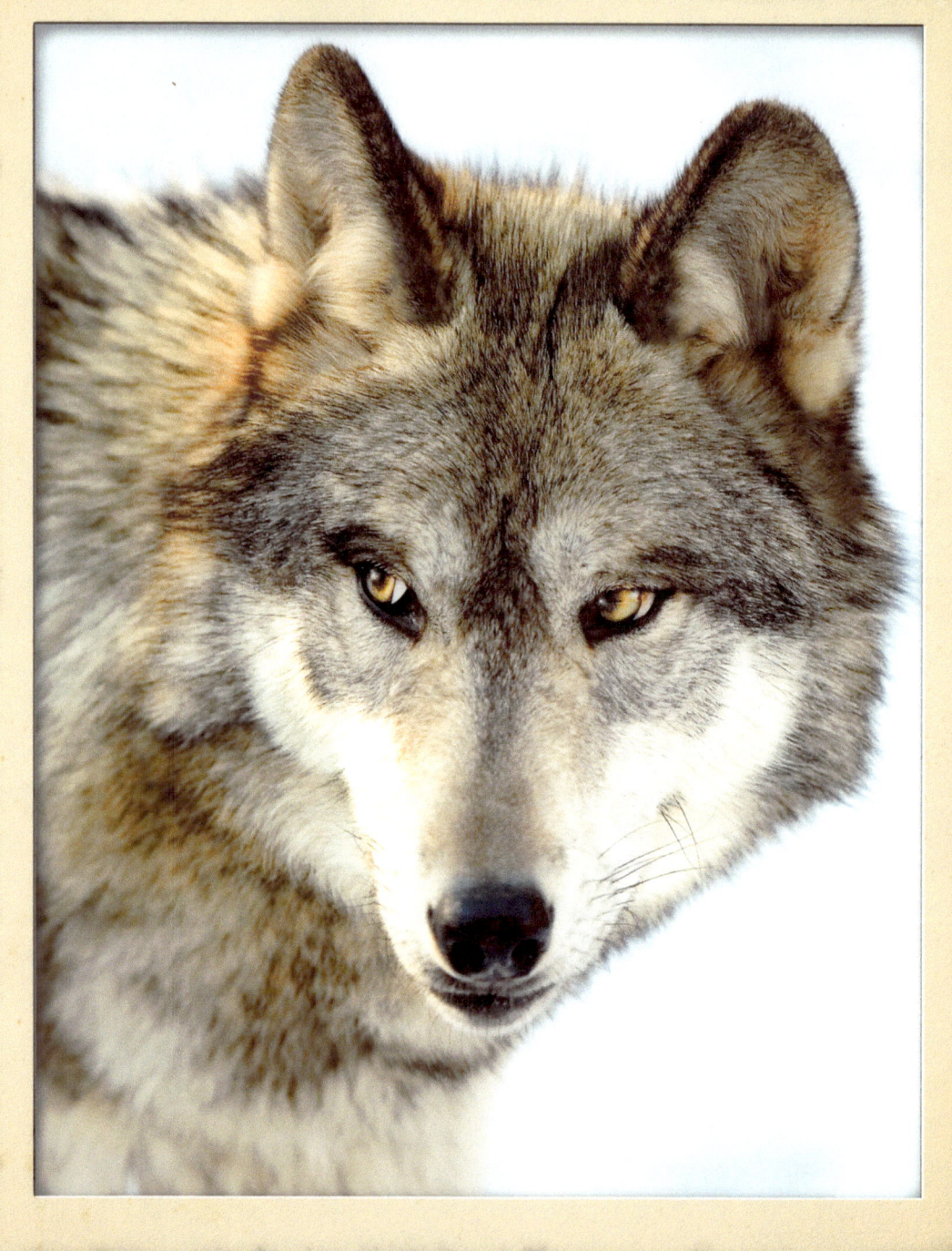

Now, if I could just find
me a sheep's costume...

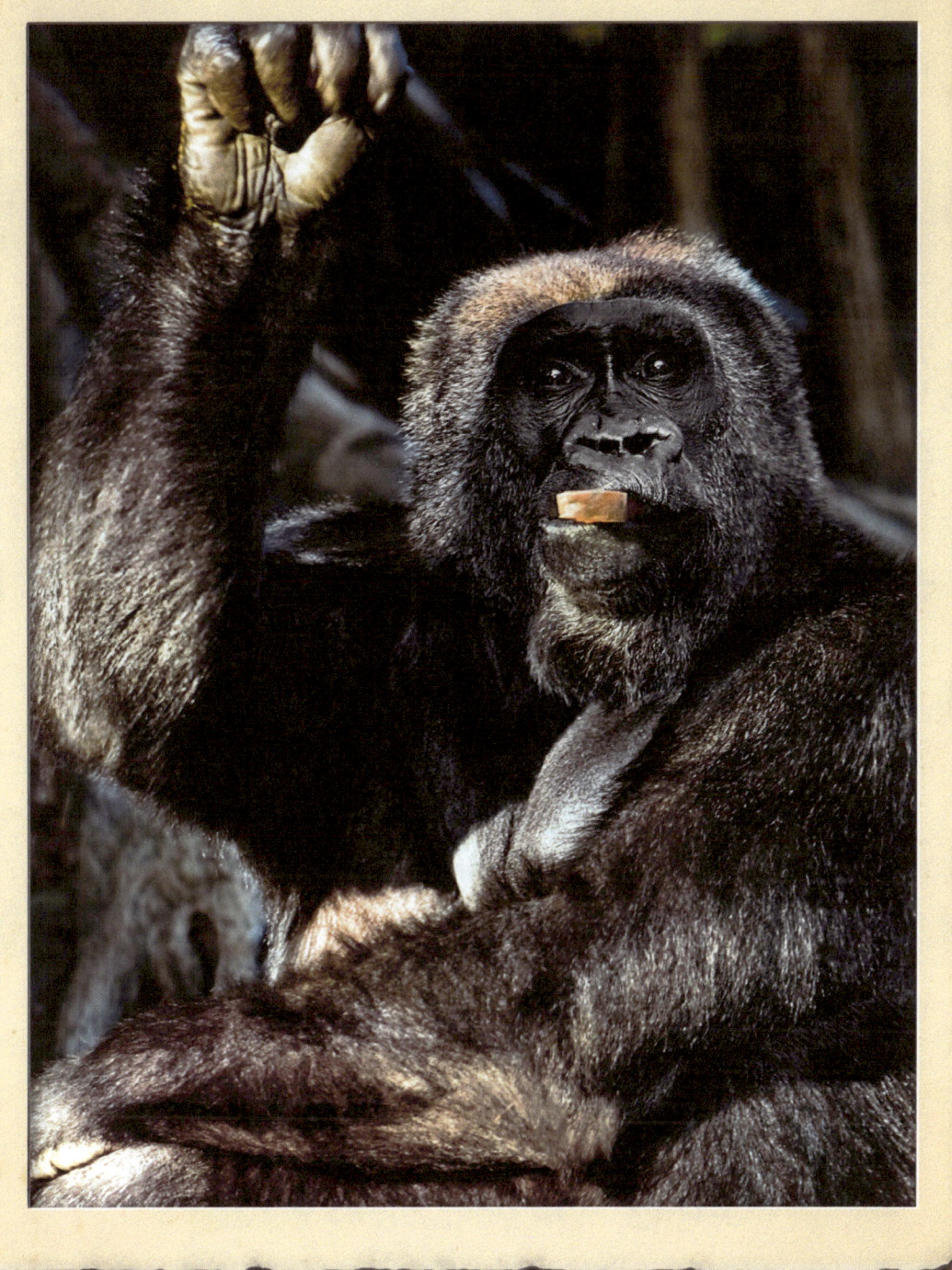

Excuuse Meee,
Mr. Zoo Keeper! This is NOT
what I ordered...

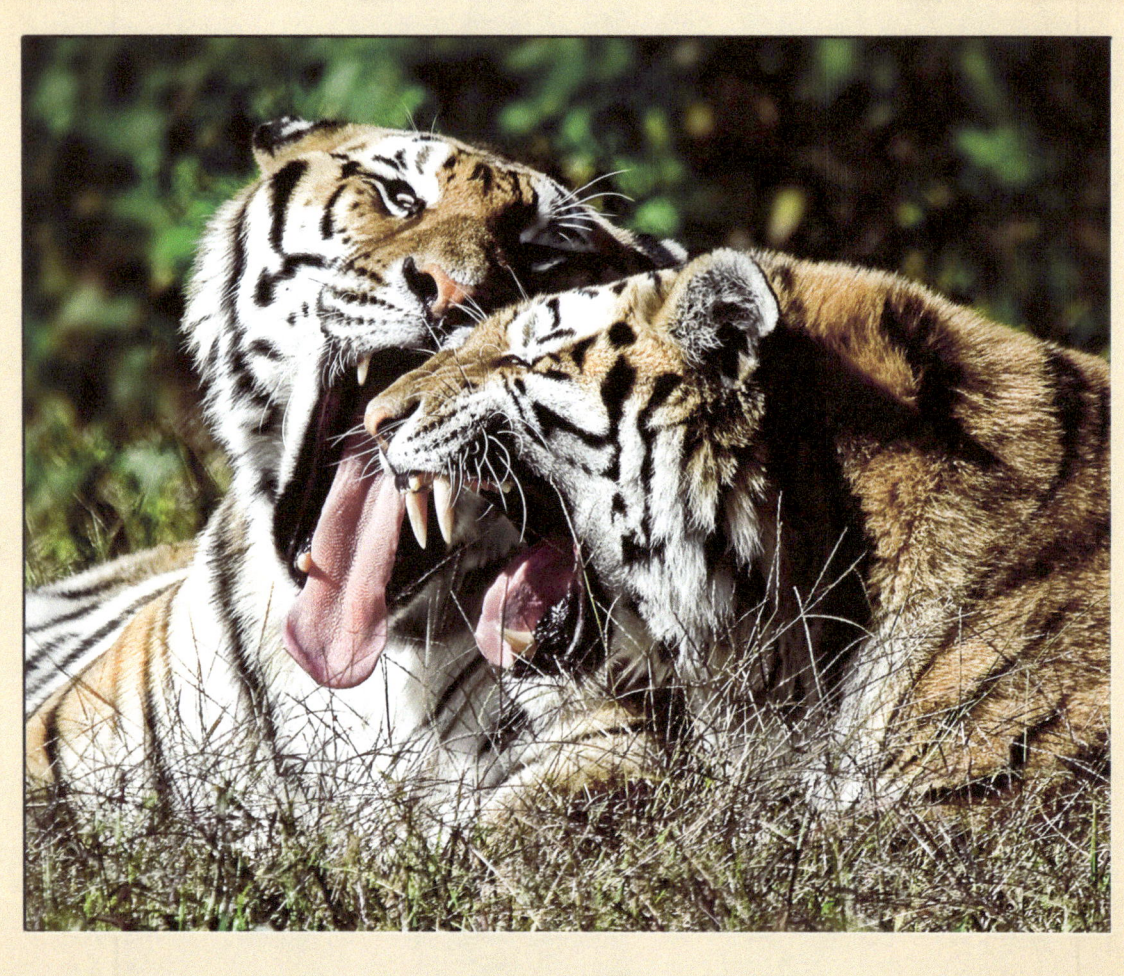

Stella, will you stop your tongue-lashing? I <u>will</u> take out the trash!

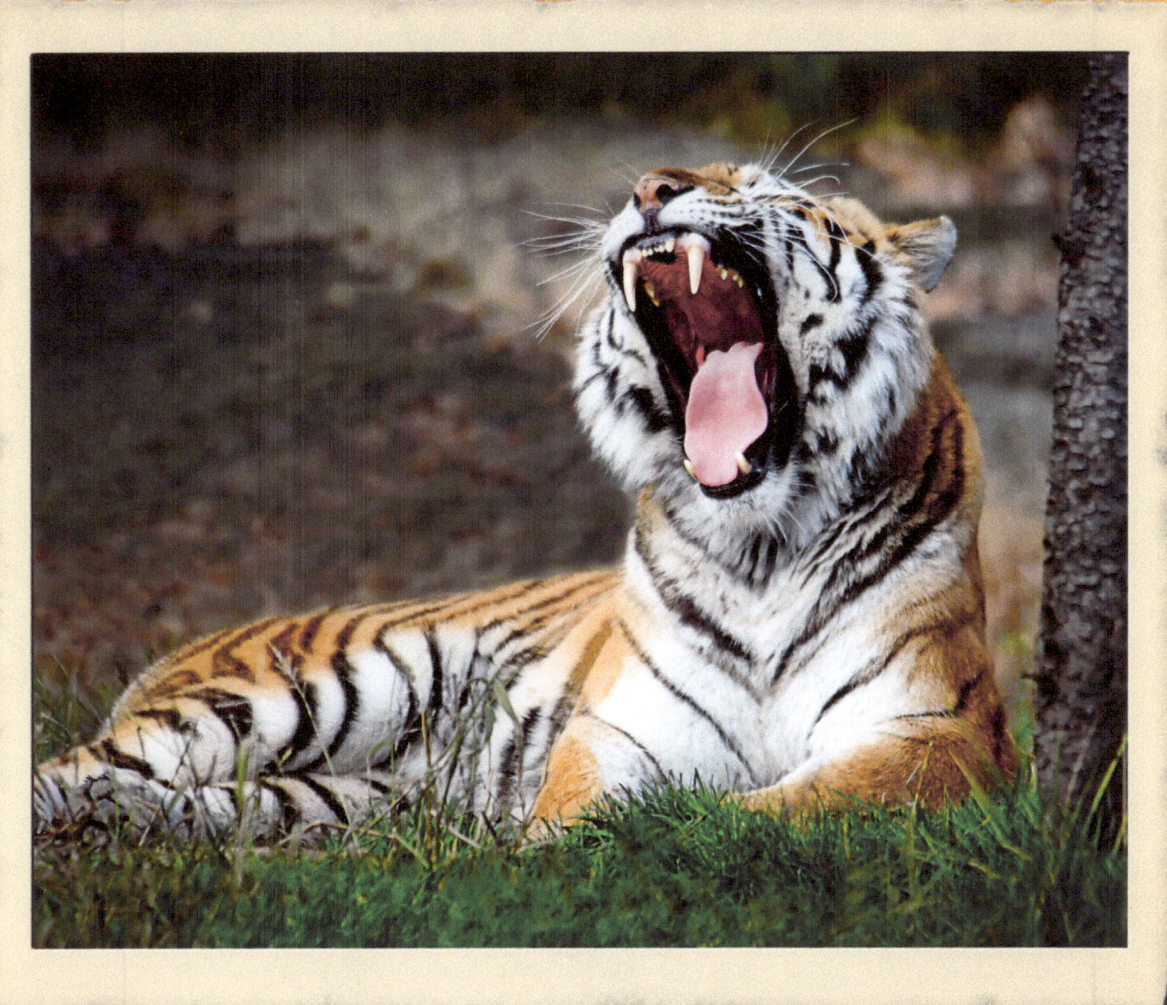

Steeeeellaaaaa ...!

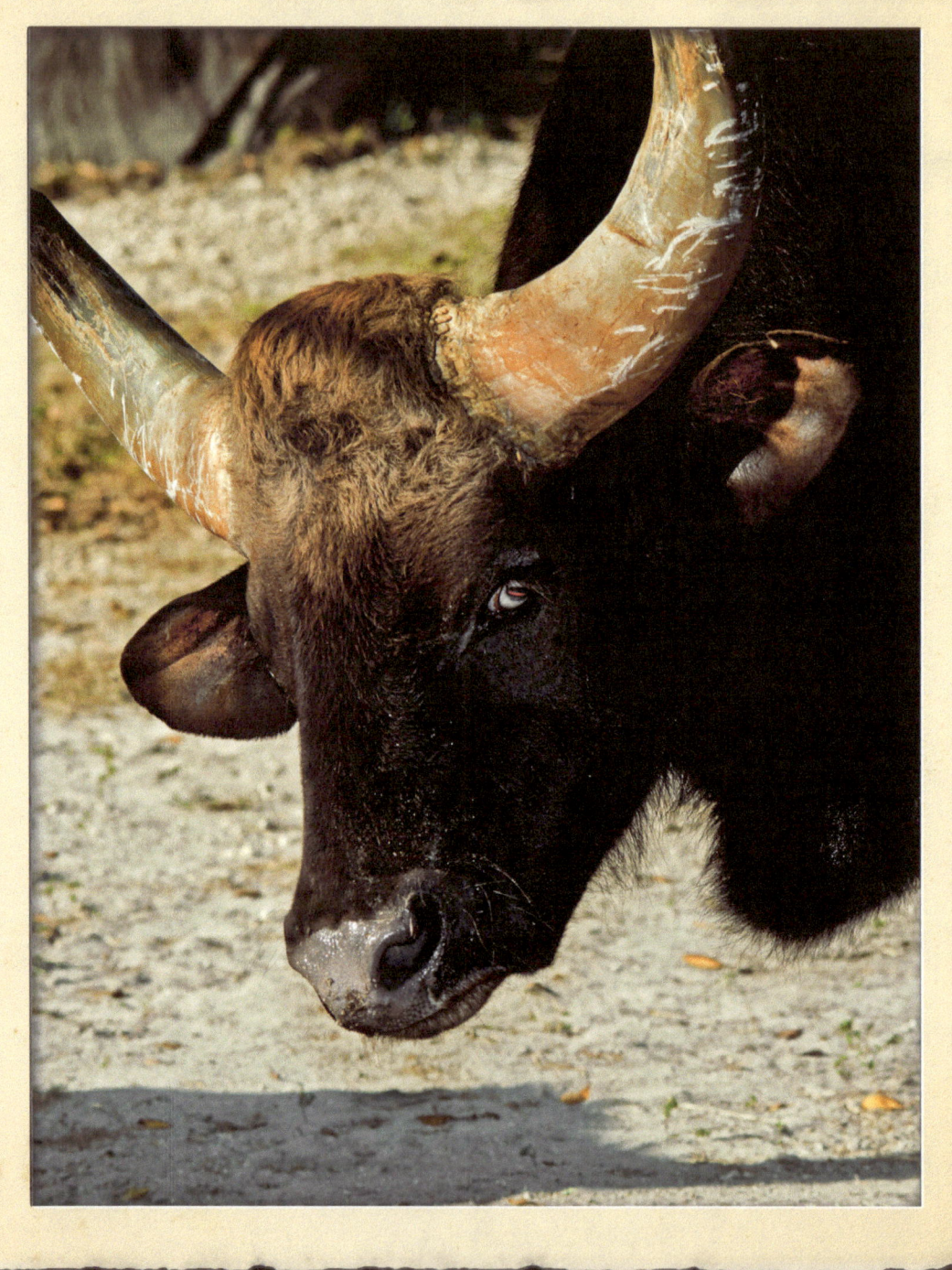

I am what I am,
...an Ungulate
gone bad...

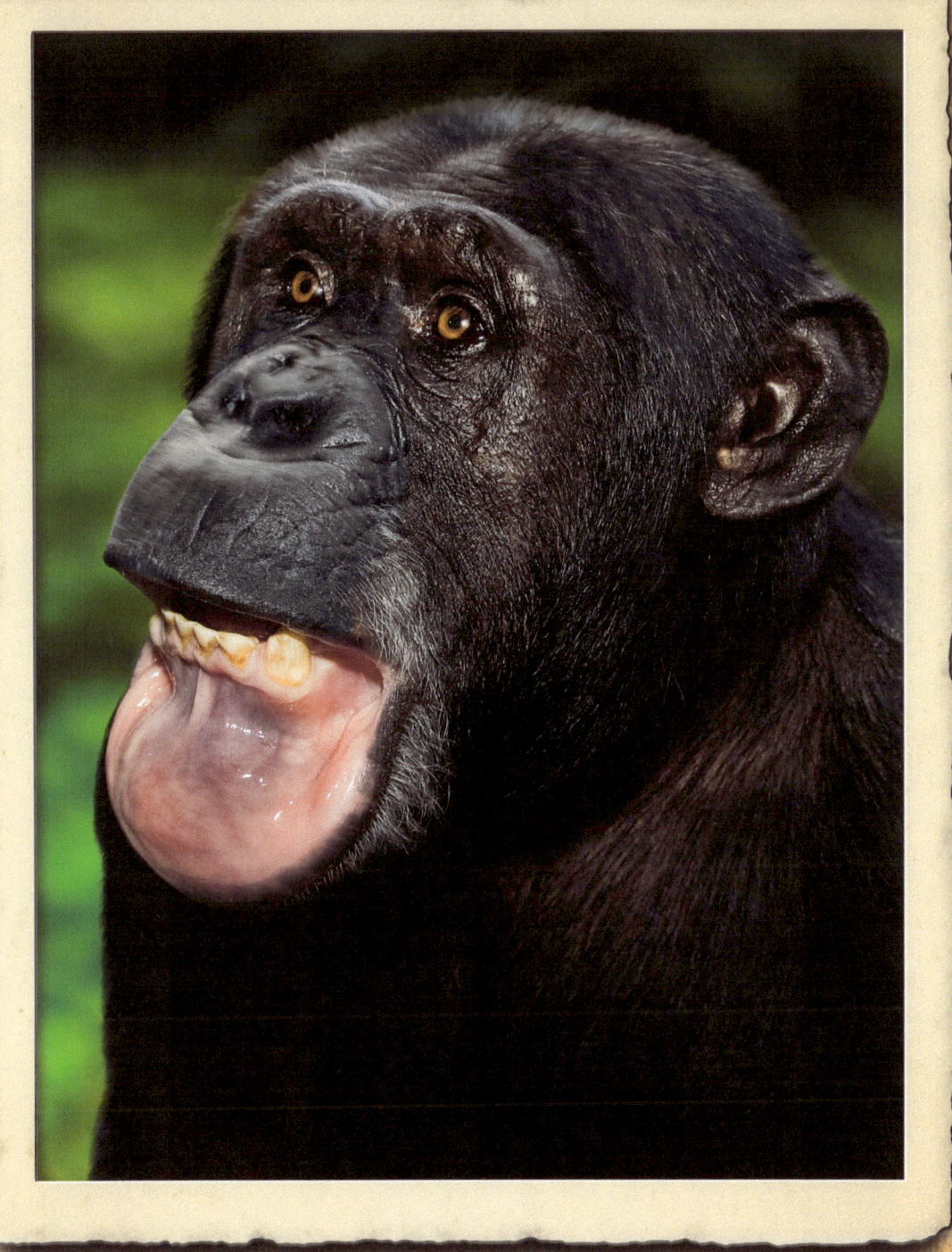

I have a feeling
I might have over done it
with the Botox...

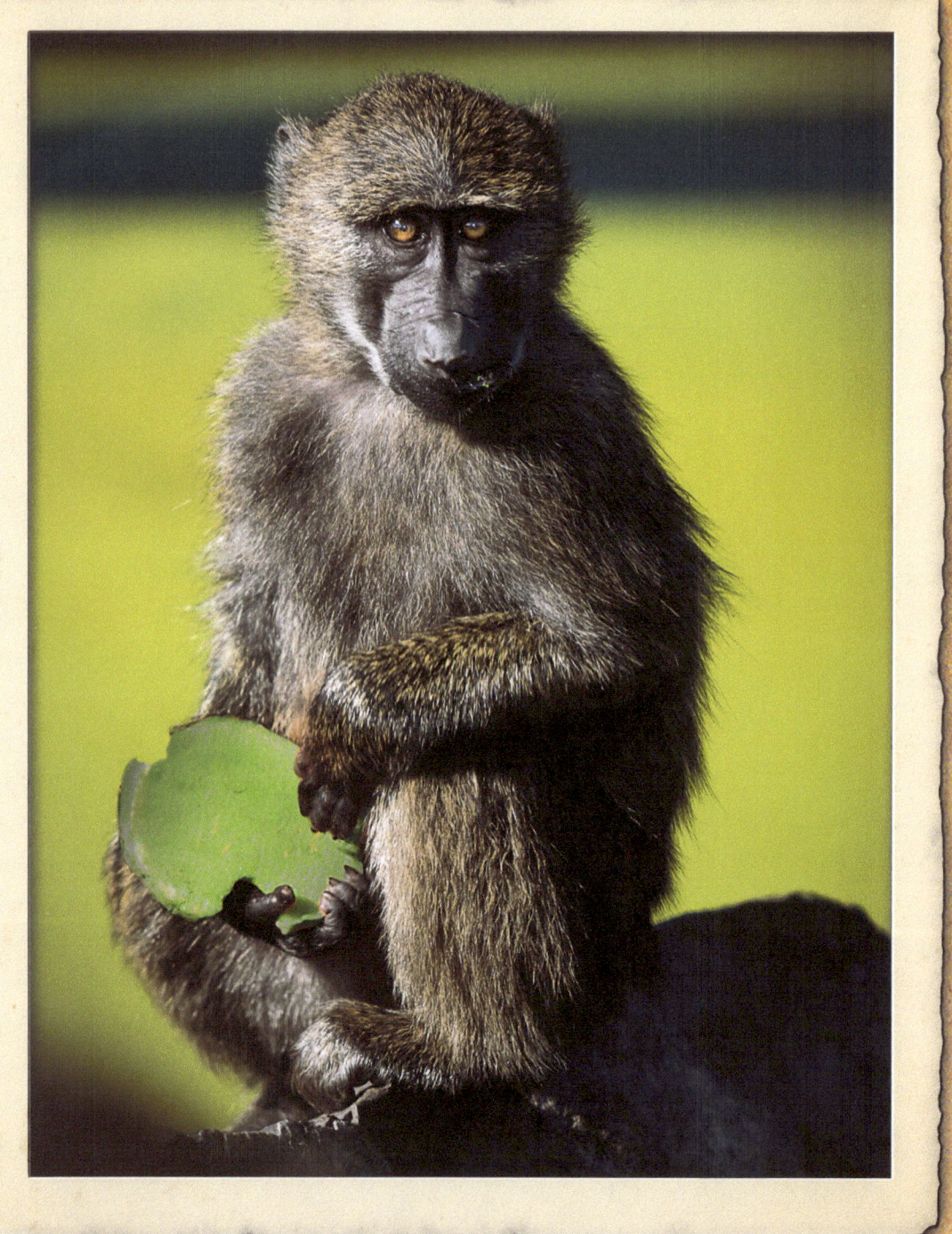

Soylent Green?
Whaddaya mean,
Soylent Green?...

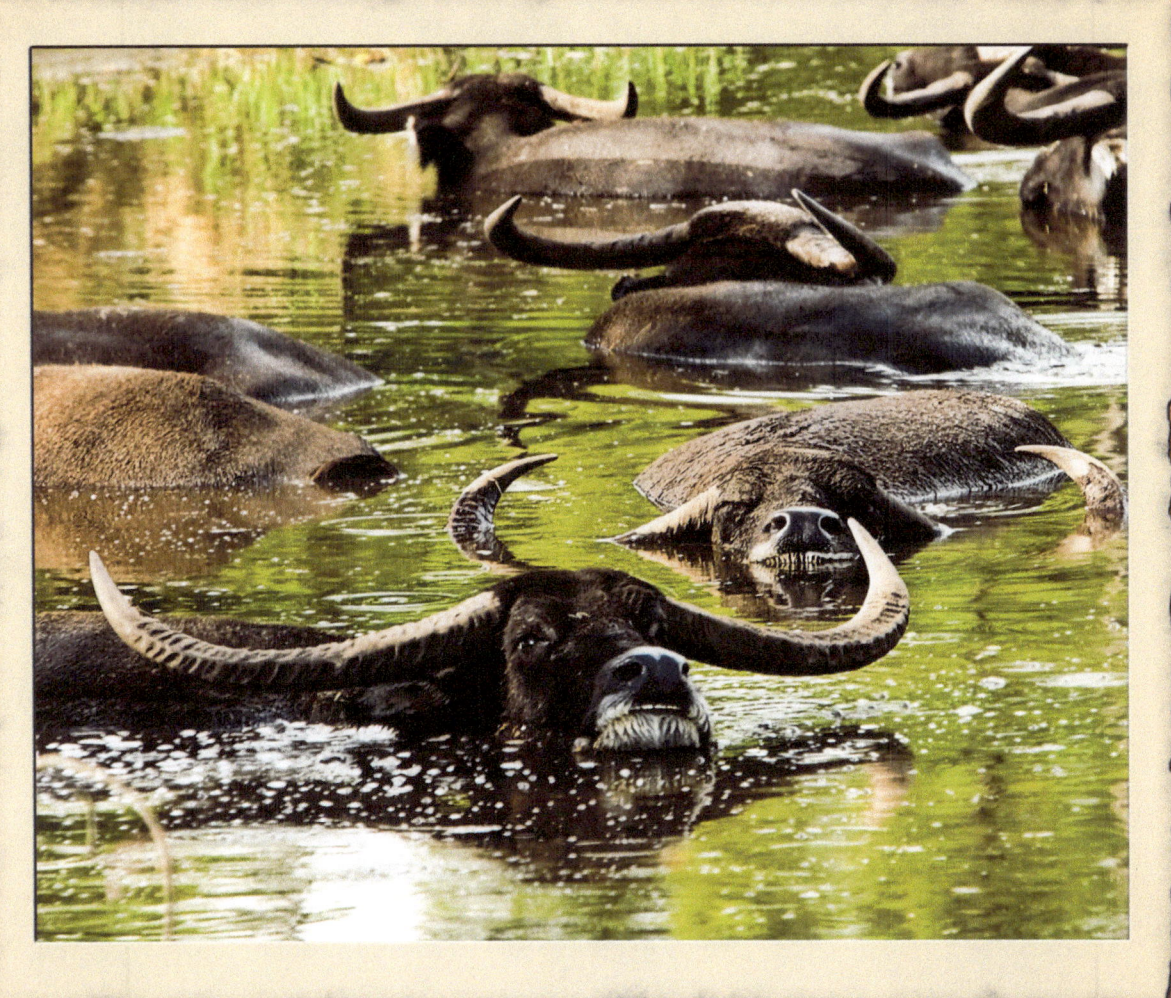

Of all the mud joints in all the
swamps of the world,
she had to wade into mine...

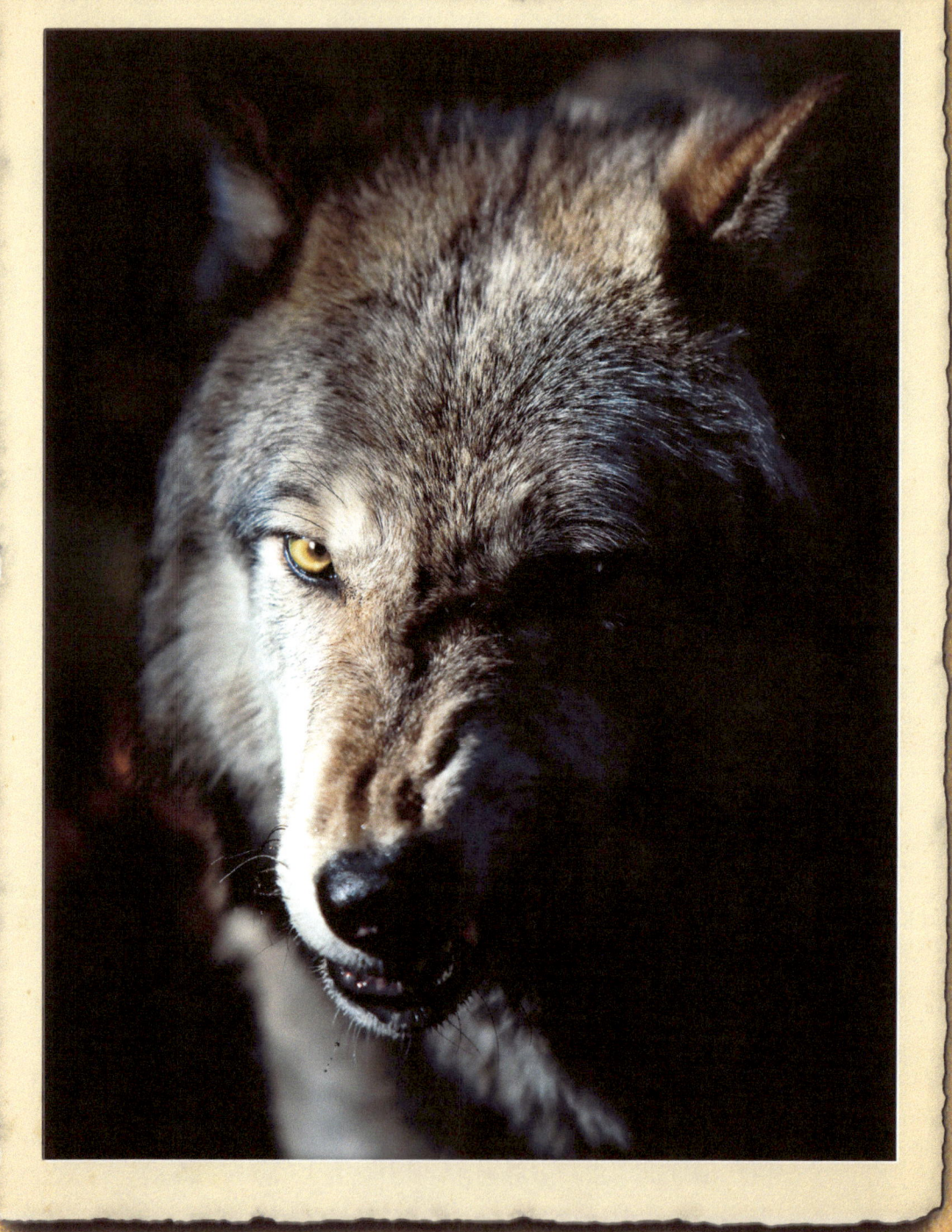

I'll huff and I'll puff...
and I'll tear
this fence down...

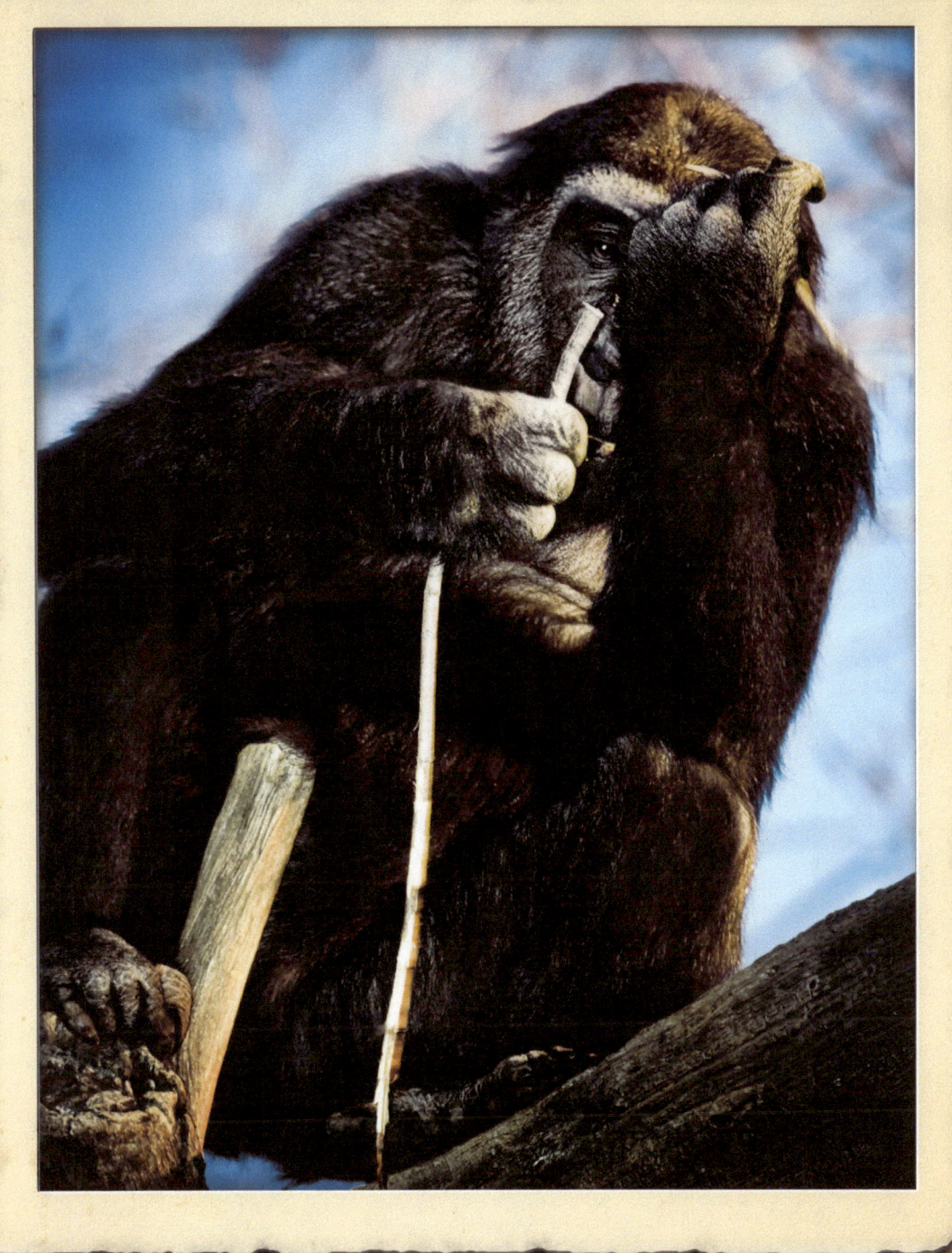

Professor Kiljoy ponders
the deep intricacies
of fire-making tools

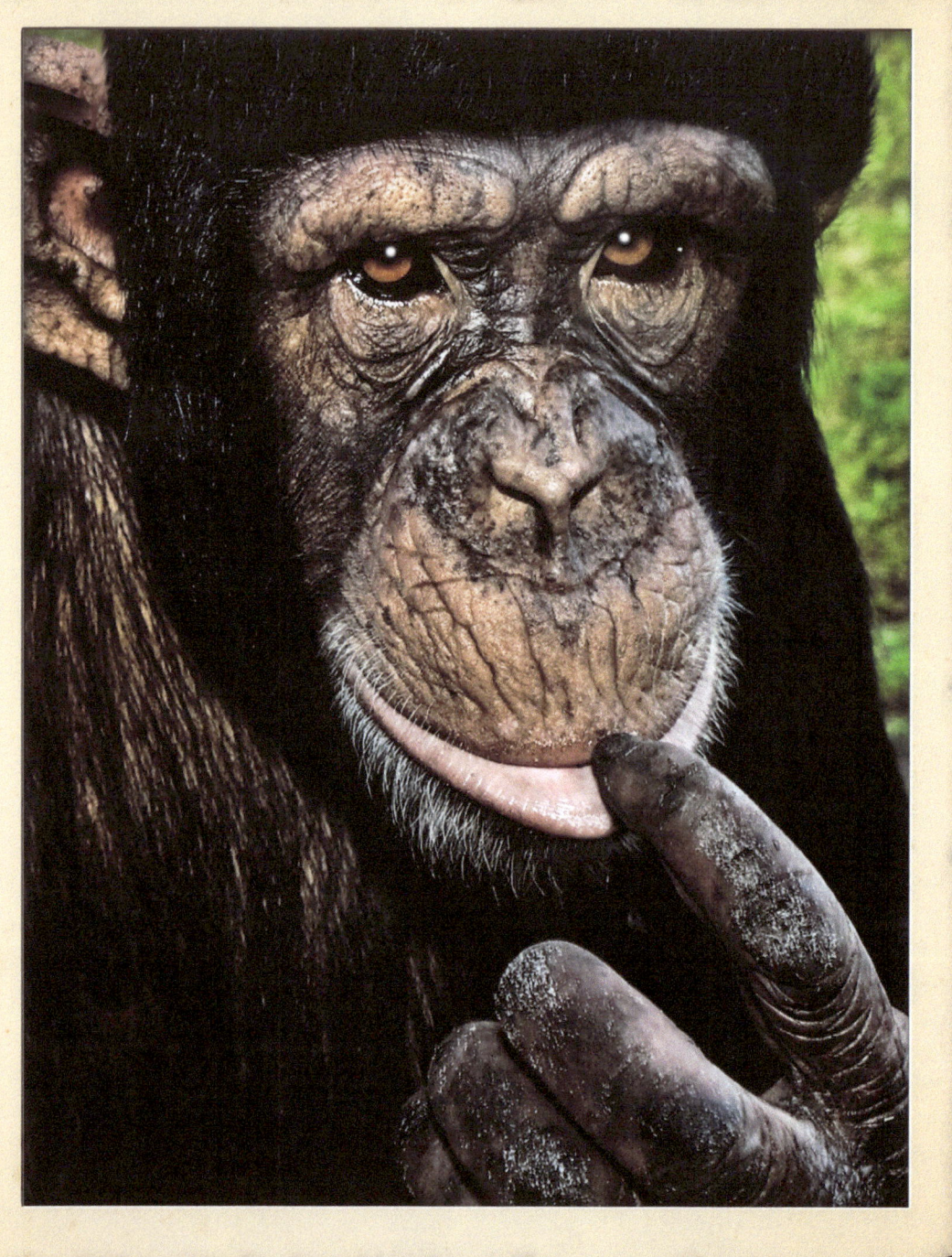

To Be or Not to Be,
That is the question...

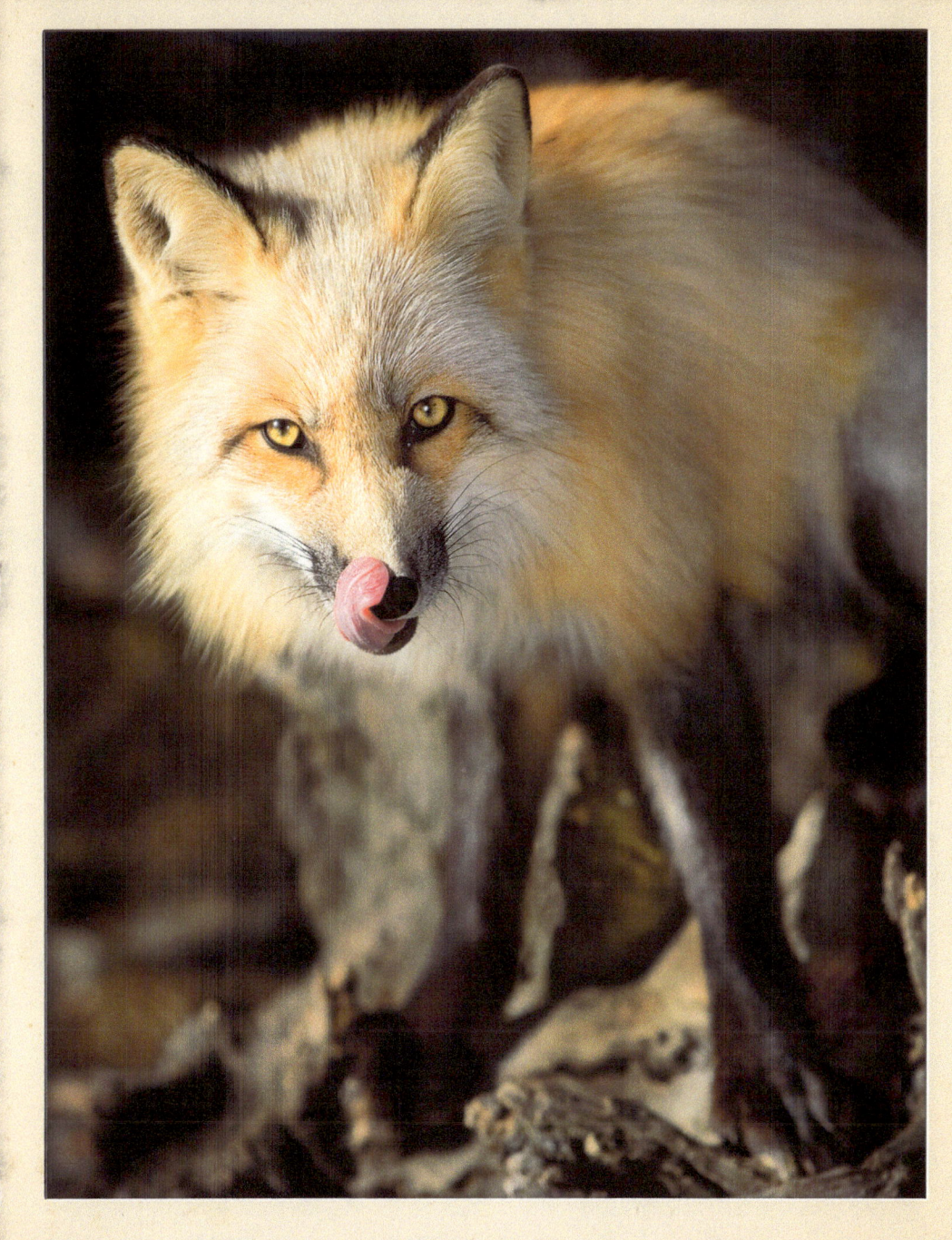

You might have noticed they rightly call me 'Foxy' you know...

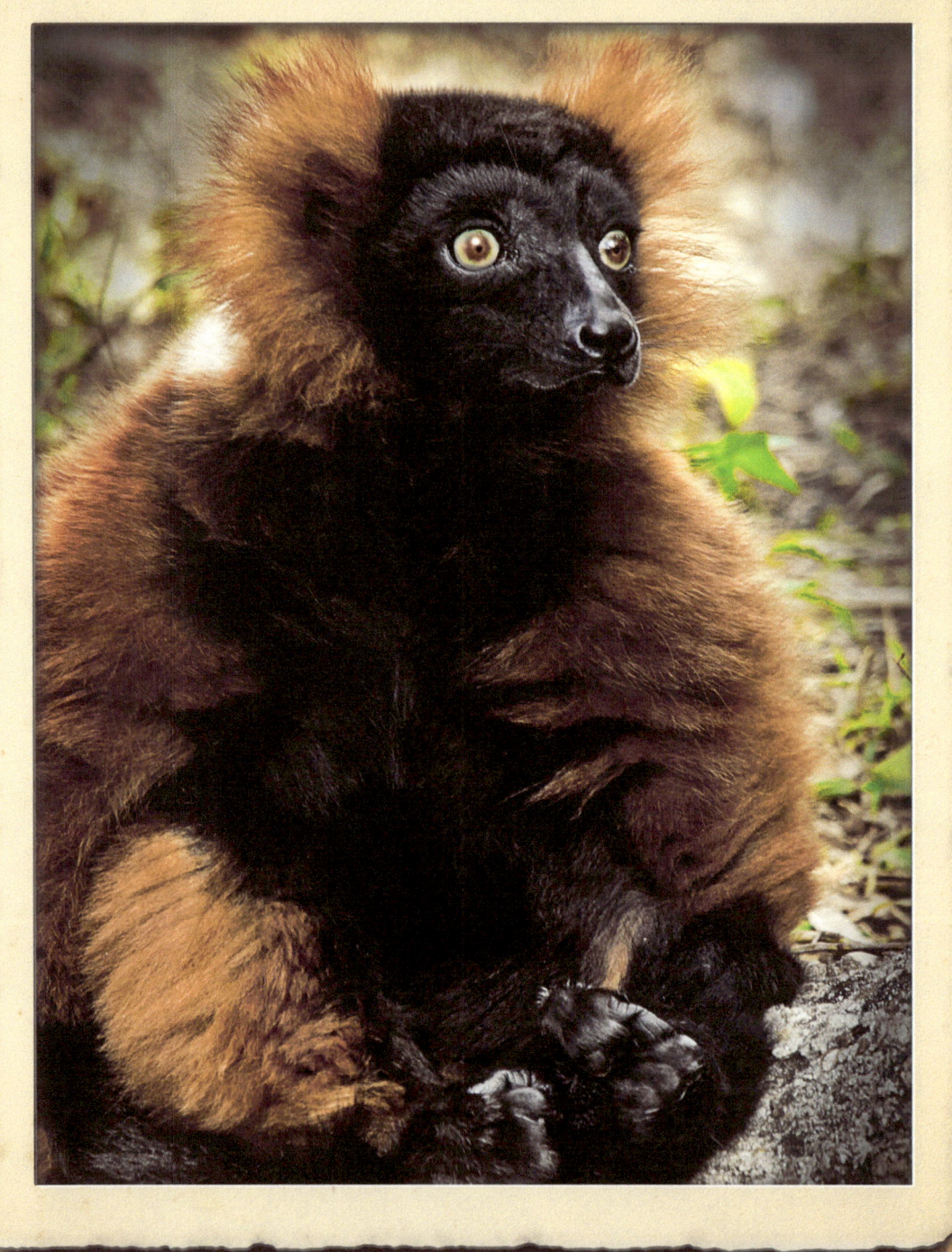

This 'survival of the fittest'
business is Stressing Me Out...

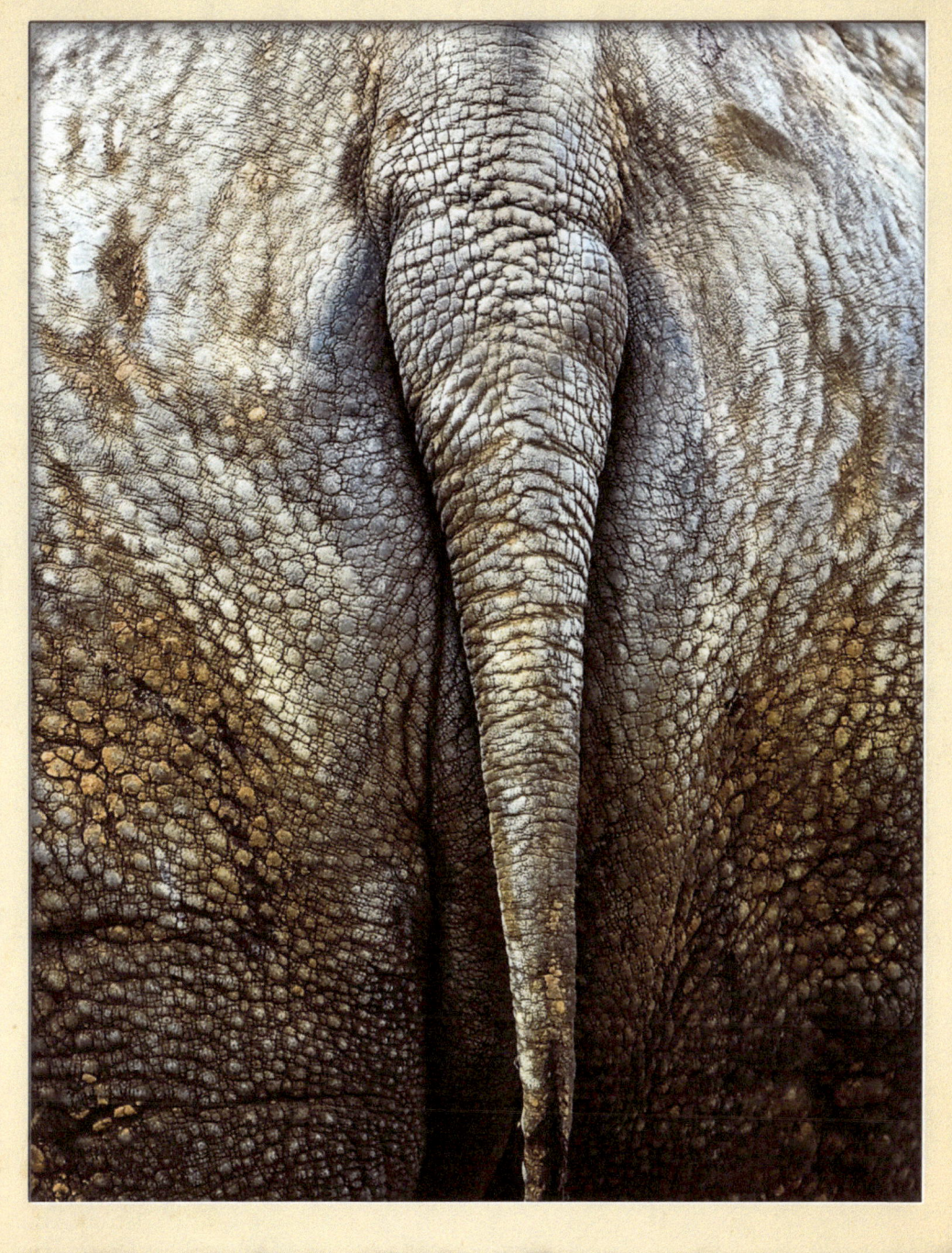

I'm a sweetheart! I just can't
see why all my friends
call me a 'Hard Ass'...

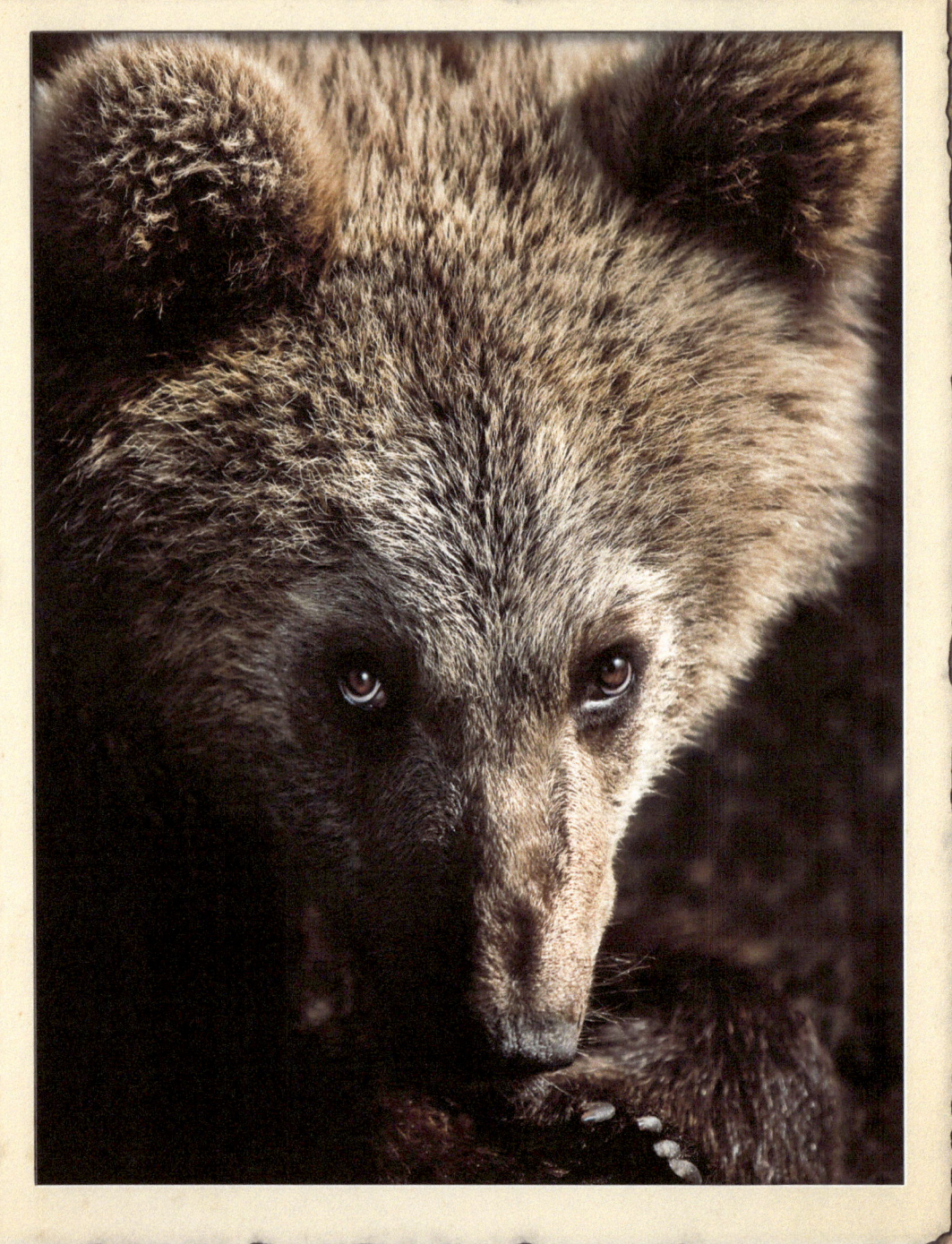

I'll pretend I'm just a cute
Teddy Bear, and when he
gets closer, Zap!...

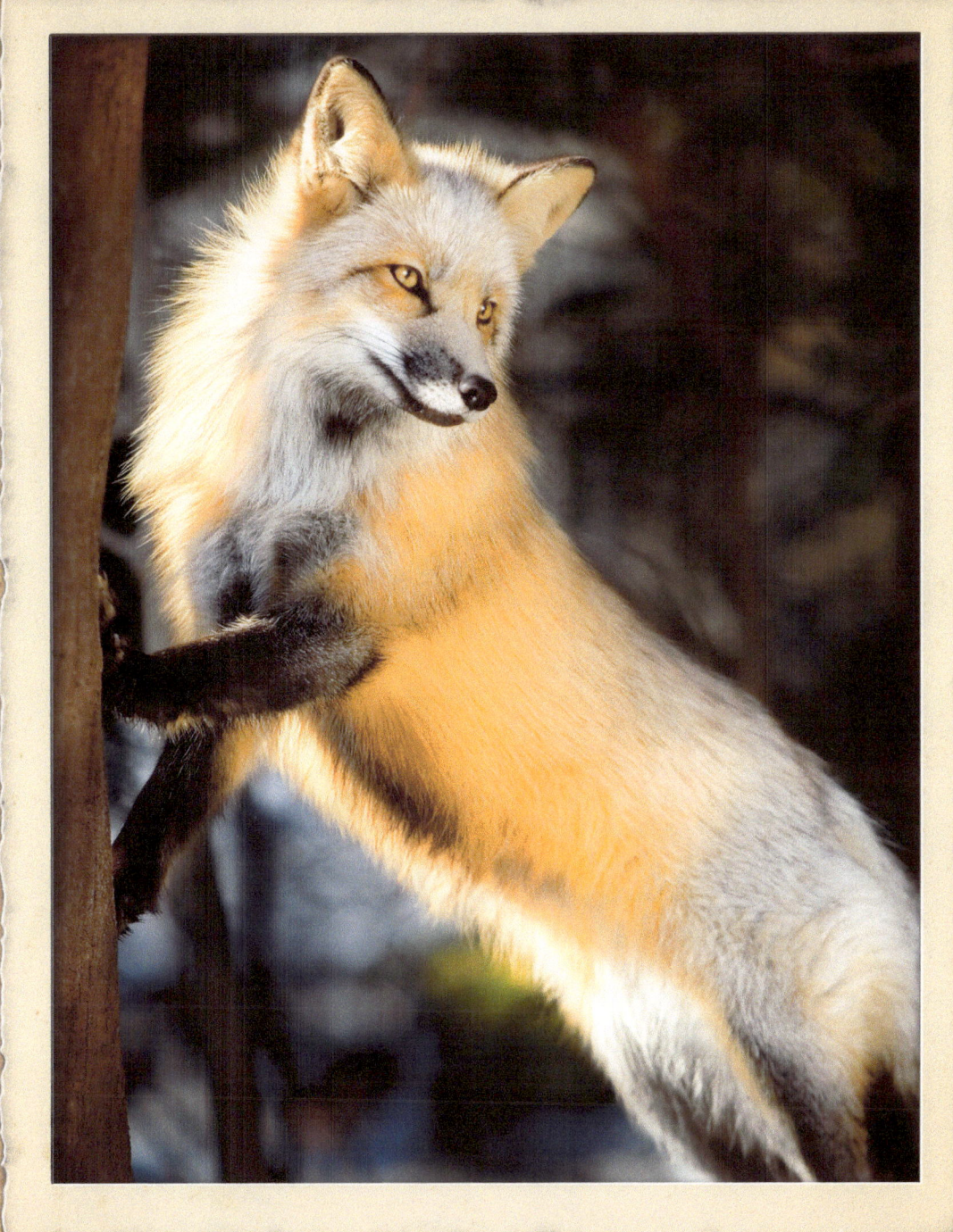

Perhaps I'll be discovered
by this photographer,
at Last!

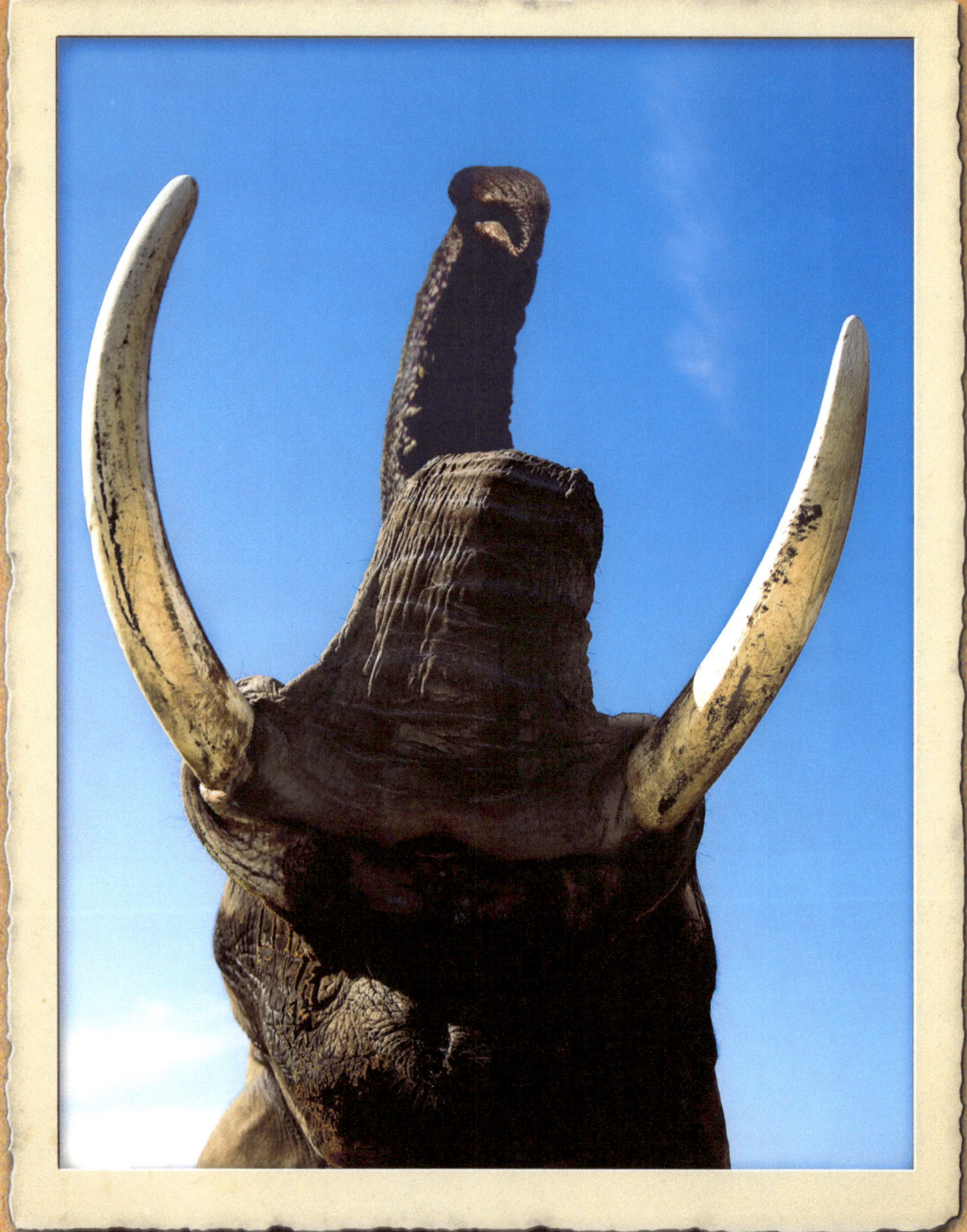

What did you just call me??
Did I hear... 'DUMBO'?!!

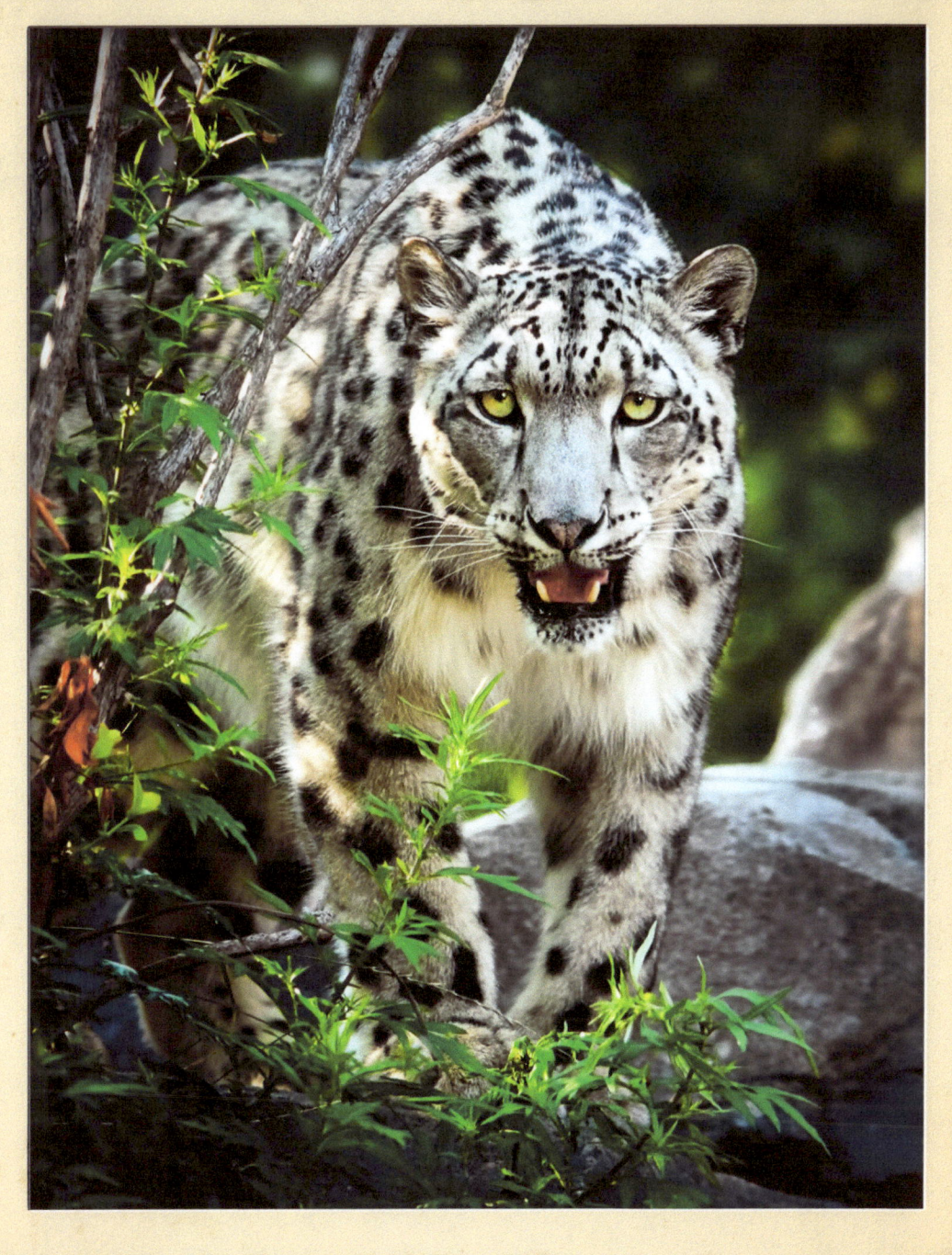

They call me a Snow
Leopard and then dump
me in this sweaty Jungle?

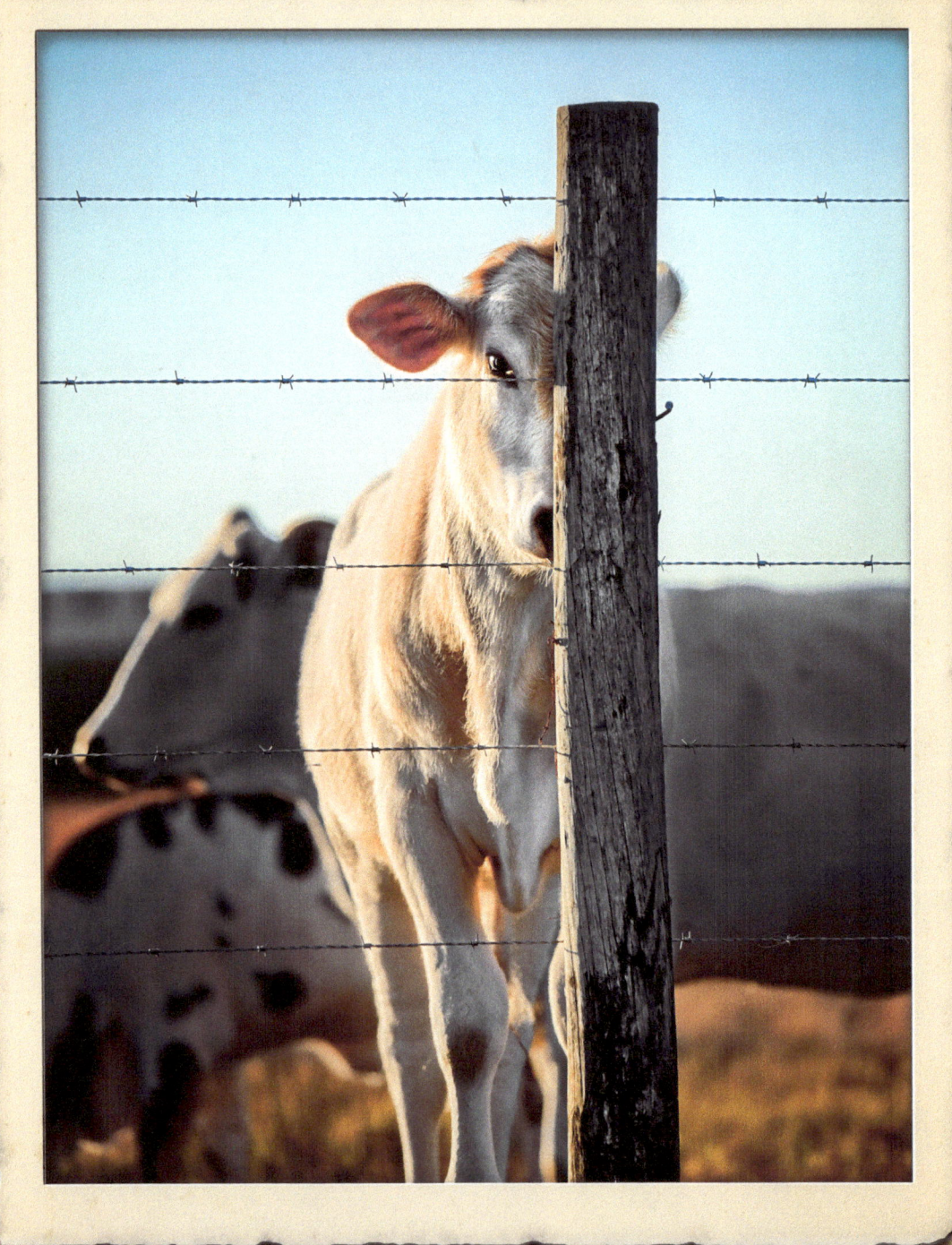

I'll stay camouflaged until the Veal Patrol leaves...

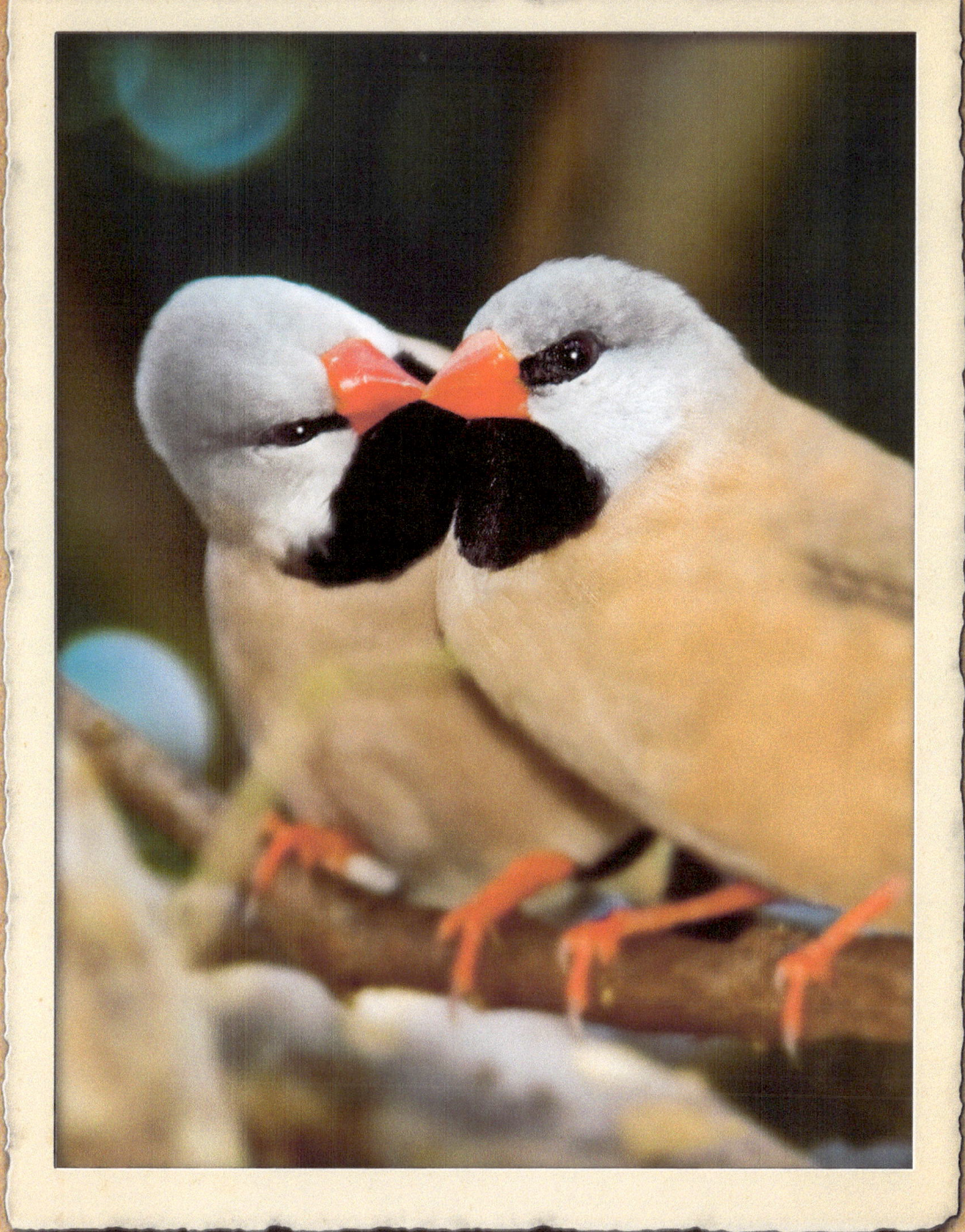

Go ahead!
Keep ignoring me, Edna...

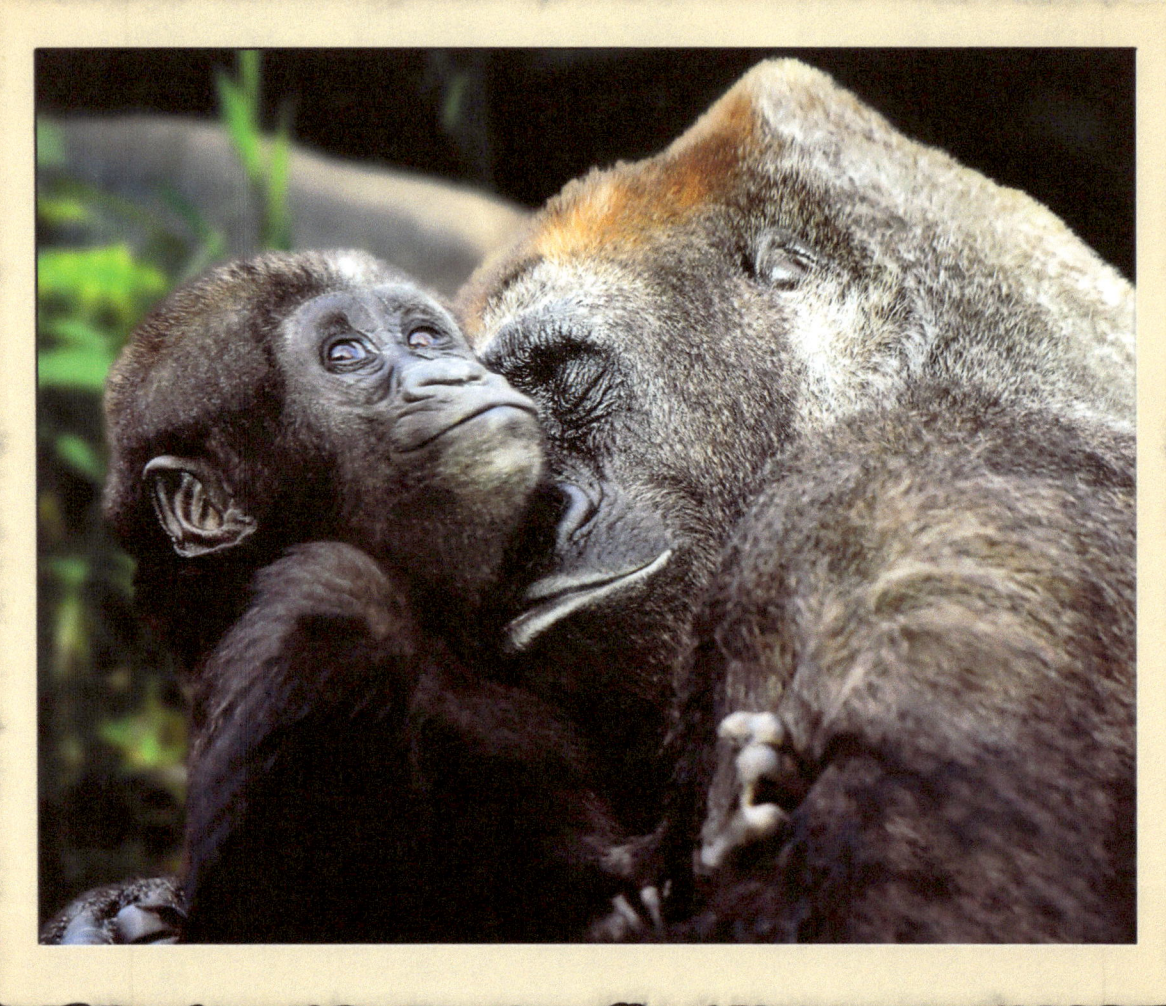

Just call me
"Spoiled Brat of the Jungle"...

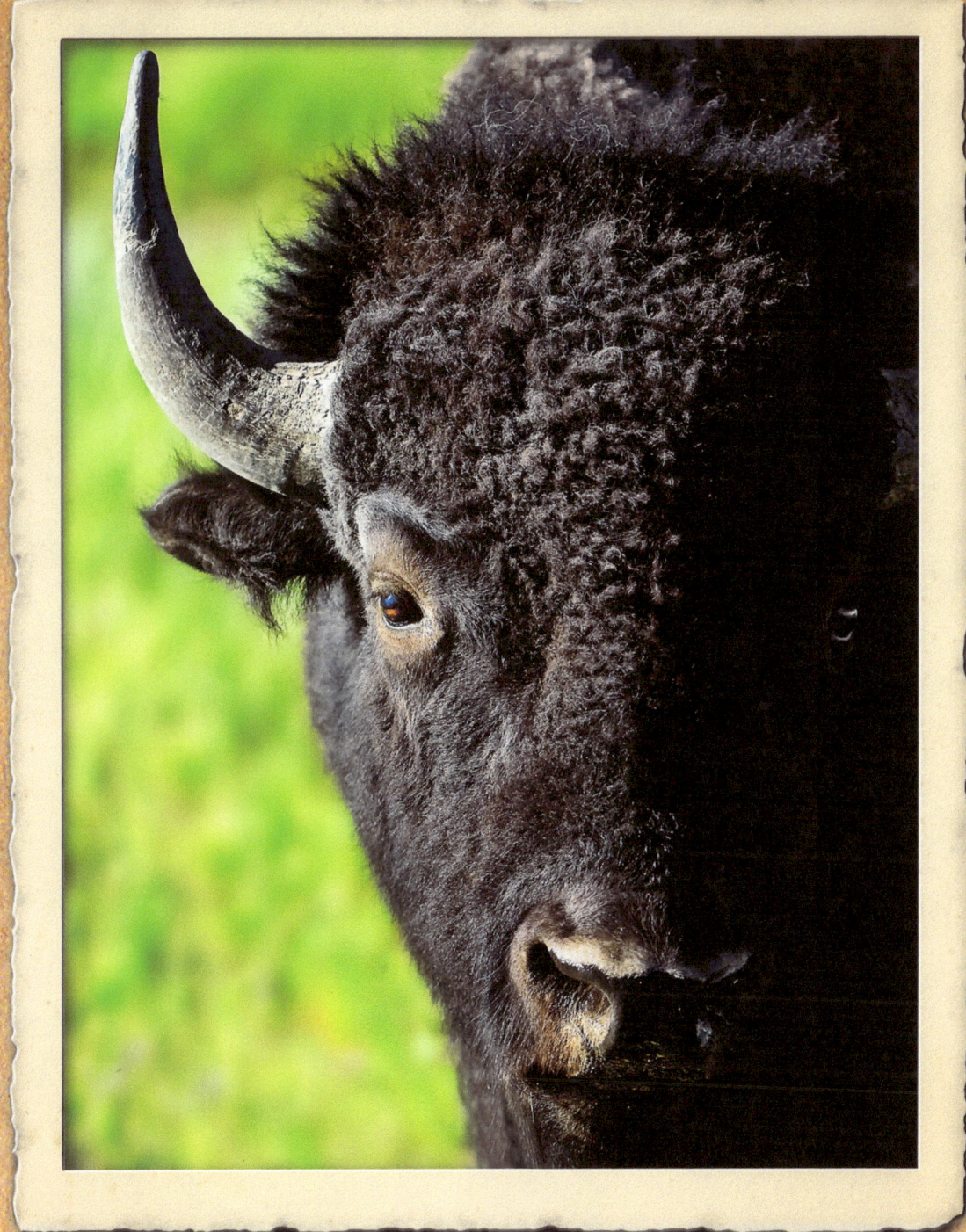

Yep, you're TOO close...

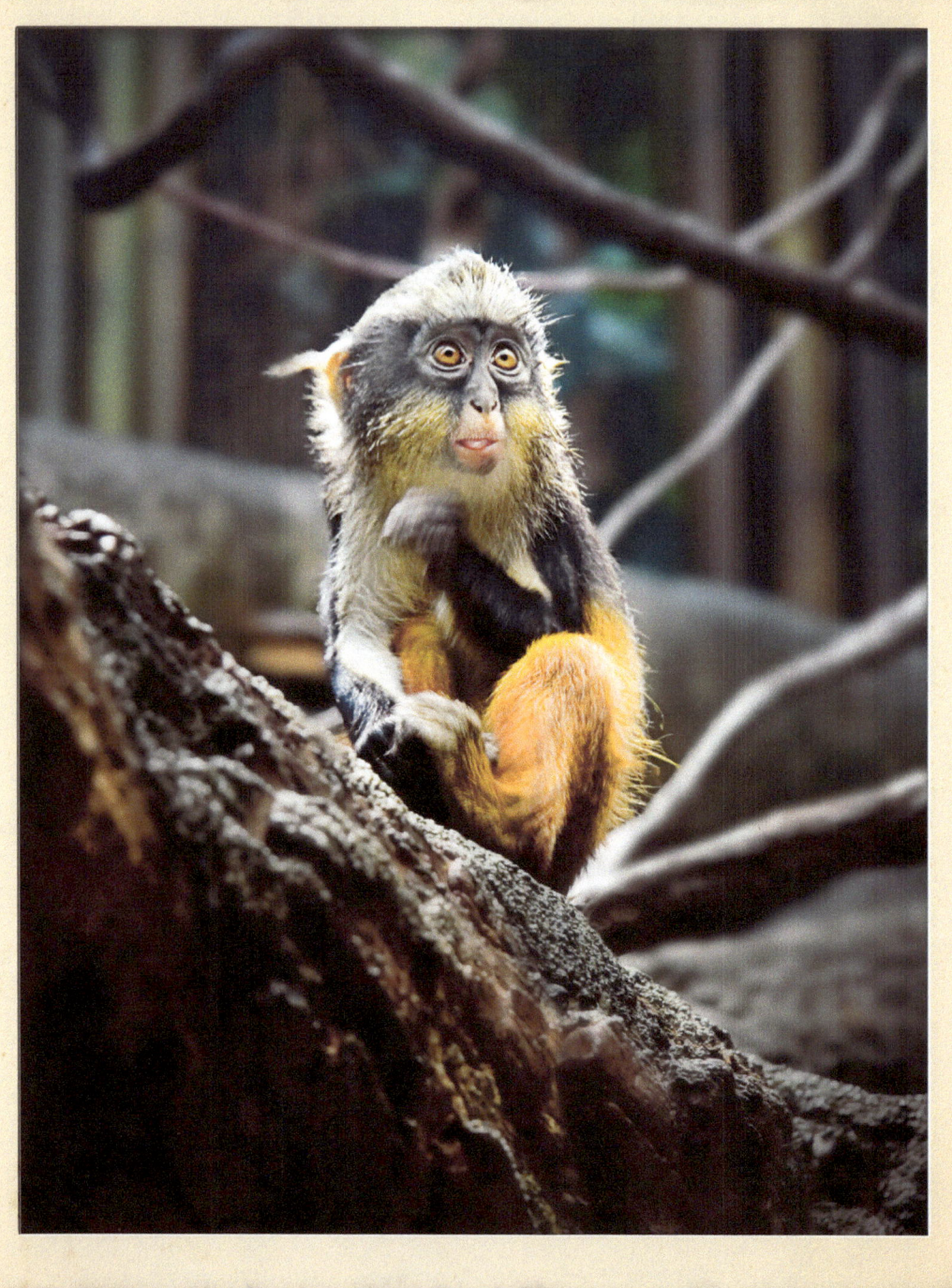

Sometimes I feel I am
diagonally parked in a
parallel universe...

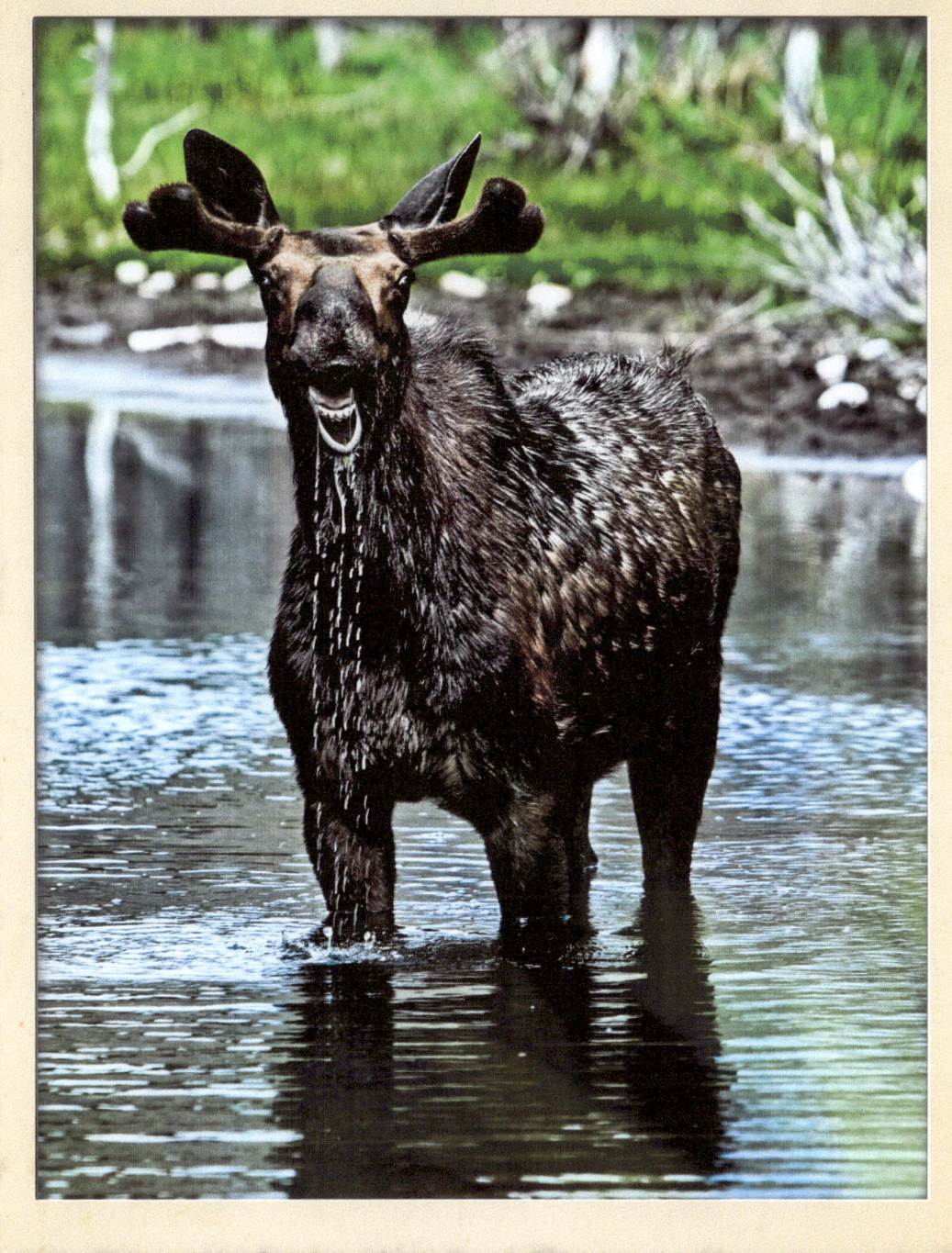

Shall I get out of
these wet furs and into
a dry martini, mmm?...